Predicting the Future with Astrology:

A Step-by-Step Guide

Predicting the Future with Astrology:

A Step-by-Step Guide

Sasha Fenton

Sterling Publishing Co., Inc.
New York

Library of Congress Cataloging-in-Publication Data Available

10 9 8 7 6 5 4 3 2 1

Published 1997 by Sterling Publishing Company, Inc.
387 Park Avenue South, New York, N.Y. 10016
Originally published in 1996 in Great Britain
by Judy Piatkus (Publishers) Ltd
Under the title *Reading the Future: A Step-by-Step Guide to Predictive Astrology*

Distributed in Canada by Sterling Publishing
℅ Canadian Manda Group, One Atlantic Avenue, Suite 105
Toronto, Ontario, Canada M6K 3E7
Manufactured in the United States of America

Sterling ISBN 0-8069-9697-8

Dedication

This book is dedicated to my friend Jonathan Dee, who is a constant source of inspiration and comfort.

Acknowledgements

If I don't acknowledge my family, they will throw me out of the house! Therefore, my thanks to the following: my super-supportive husband Tony, without whom we would all either live on takeouts or starve! My daughter Helen, who makes all my journeys smooth. My Son Stuart, without whom I would be completely computer-illiterate, and my daughter-in-law Maria, who cheers me up by popping in for chats and doing the odd bit of proof-reading at the same time.

To Jonathan Dee for the illustrations and many useful ideas in this book. Also for the use of his partner's chart. Thanks Jon for your constant faith in my abilities when my own faith wanes.

To Denise Stuart and Anne Christie, without whom I couldn't get through the trials and tribulations of my life. Also for the charts and the stories that they have allowed me to use depicting some of *their* trials and tribulations.

To Martin Davis of Matrix UK, for computing information and his amazingly educational form of friendship. To Roy Gillett of the Roy Gillett Consultancy, for being patient, kind and helpful and for supplying me with computer information. Also for allowing me to use the Solar Fire charts in this book. Both have kindly helped by supplying the technical details in Chapter 6.

To all the many friends and colleagues who have popped up with useful bits and pieces, especially Douglas Ashby, Nina Ashby, Kathy Fay, Maggie Hyde and another new pal, Andy Pancholi.

With gratitude to HarperCollins for allowing me to use material from my book *Rising Signs*.

Contents

all the planetary movements. This will enable you to make an immediate start on discovering what the forthcoming aspects in your horoscope may bring – and perhaps help to keep you out of trouble too. If you, dear reader, discover the secret of avoiding the wrath of the planetary gods, perhaps you could let me into it!

A word about etiquette

If you progress to reading for clients, you will need to combine sensitivity, honesty and common sense. There is no point in alarming a friend or client by stressing the negative items on a horoscope but on the other hand, there is no point in telling them what they want to hear just to keep them happy. If you are not sure about the potential outcome of a particular planetary movement, make a few suggestions and leave it there. If you need inspiration, there is nothing shameful in getting an astrology book from your shelf and looking something up. Lawyers, doctors and other professionals consult books in front of their clients, so why not you? Nobody can know it all and even those who have come across everything in astrology at some time or another cannot remember it all.

The choices people make about their love lives, their careers or anything else are their own. There is nothing wrong with making helpful suggestions or pointing out potential pitfalls, but you can't wave a magic wand and make another person's hard times disappear. There is no nicer feeling than helping someone to see themselves and their situation clearly and allowing them to come to useful and sensible decisions. However, the world is full of people whose motives are suspect or who are determined to give themselves a hard time. You can make a few gentle suggestions but if they are bent on destruction or self-destruction, there is nothing you can do.

Some astrologers consider that you shouldn't even consider giving a reading without becoming a qualified psychotherapist or counsellor but there is no need for this. Your job is not to take on all the craziness in the world but to enlighten others in a pleasant and even an entertaining manner. There is a limit to what others should expect of you. You also need to accept that you will never be totally accurate in your judgement, and even when you do get it all absolutely right, your client may very well defy whatever is showing up on his or her chart. Free-will always overcomes fate. You are only a human being, you are not divine!

Part One

First Steps for Beginners

1

If You Know Nothing about Astrology, Start Here

Sun signs

IF YOU NEED to check out your own Sun sign, look at the following list, which I have taken from *Woman's Own* magazine:

Aries March 21 to April 20
Taurus April 21 to May 21
Gemini May 22 to June 21
Cancer June 22 to July 23
Leo July 24 to August 23
Virgo August 24 to September 23
Libra September 24 to October 23
Scorpio October 24 to November 22
Sagittarius November 23 to December 21
Capricorn December 22 to January 20
Aquarius January 21 to February 19
Pisces February 20 to March 20

Sun sign dates differ from one magazine or paper to another because the Sun doesn't automatically change sign at the same time or even on the same day of each year. If you were born on the cusp, that is to say, where two signs meet, you may need to find out what *time* you were born, because it is quite possible for a person born in the morning of a particular day to have a different Sun sign to someone who was born a bit later. Even twins can have different Sun signs!

People often ask if being born close to another sign means that their characters are influenced by the adjacent sign. Some astrologers think that this is so, while others are equally adamant that it is not. Anyway, there are so many other factors to take into account on a birthchart that a 'cuspy' Sun would not count much to an astrologer. There are astrologers who won't even accept the term 'cusp', suggesting that each of us quite definitely has the Sun in one sign or another.

Timing of events

Now that you know what Sun sign you were born under, forget it for a while and look at the calendar instead! There are certain times of the year when things go well for all of us, and other times when they can be almost guaranteed to go wrong. Some people always have a terrible Christmas, while others dread the summer. The calendars pictured in this chapter will help you to find those months that are likely to be harmonious or difficult for you.

Generally speaking, most people have mixed feelings about life around the time of their birthdays. We all enjoy receiving cards and presents but we hate getting older, and we may look back and consider that we haven't achieved all that we should so far. These mixed feelings are typical of a planetary *conjunction*, that is, where the planets up in the sky are crossing the path of those on our own horoscopes. At the time of your birthday, a number of planets will be passing close by the place where the Sun (as well as Mercury or Venus) was when you were born. If you write down the months of the year on a piece of paper in a circular or 'clock' form, you will immediately be able to find the month that is *opposite* to your own birth month, which will be six months after your own birth month. This is likely to be a 'down' time, when you will feel ill and out of sorts. You may be 'up to your neck in things' when the Sun is *square* to your own birth month, these times being three or nine months after your own birth month. On the other hand, you should feel in command of yourself and your life when the Sun is two, four, eight or ten months away from your birthday.

An even simpler way of looking at this

Take a look at the example on page 6 (figure 1). This is for someone born in the month of May and it shows you how to use the system. The second version is for you to use for yourself. If you can bring yourself to desecrate this book, pencil in your month of birth in the first box followed by all the other months. If you cannot face writing in a book, photocopy this page instead. You will probably be breaking a whole pile of copyright laws, but if you don't say anything, neither will I!

The astrologer's calendar

Just as the months on a calendar always begin with January and end in December, so the zodiac signs always start with Aries and end with Pisces (as per the list below). This time, therefore, put your *own* zodiac sign in the first box in figure 2 and then follow on downwards with all the succeeding ones. The following list shows the order of the signs of the zodiac.

Aries ♈
Taurus ♉
Gemini ♊
Cancer ♋
Leo ♌
Virgo ♍
Libra ♎
Scorpio ♏
Sagittarius ♐
Capricorn ♑
Aquarius ♒
Pisces ♓

MONTH	STATUS
May	Important
June	Pleasant
July	Excellent
August	Difficult
September	Excellent
October	Awkward
November	Challenging
December	Troublesome
January	Excellent
February	Difficult
March	Excellent
April	Depressing

Figure 1 The Calendar Box
The above example is for someone born in May

While the calendar box will suggest which are your better and worse months, the zodiac box will demonstrate the times of the year when you are feeling good or down-hearted – the difference being merely in the terminology. A non-astrologer might say, 'I always have a good September', an astrologer might say, 'I am at my best when the Sun is in Virgo.'

MONTH	STATUS
	Important
	Pleasant
	Excellent
	Difficult
	Excellent
	Awkward
	Challenging
	Troublesome
	Excellent
	Difficult
	Excellent
	Depressing

Your Calendar Box
Place your own birth month in the top box and then follow on downwards with all the succeeding months

Now, if you express these boxes as a clock-shaped circle (see figure 3 on page 9), with your birth month on the left-hand side in the eight o'clock position, you will begin to think like an astrologer.

MONTH	STATUS
	Important
	Pleasant
	Excellent
	Difficult
	Excellent
	Awkward
	Challenging
	Troublesome
	Excellent
	Difficult
	Excellent
	Depressing

Figure 2 The Zodiac Box
Simply place your own zodiac sign in the top box and then follow on downwards with all the rest

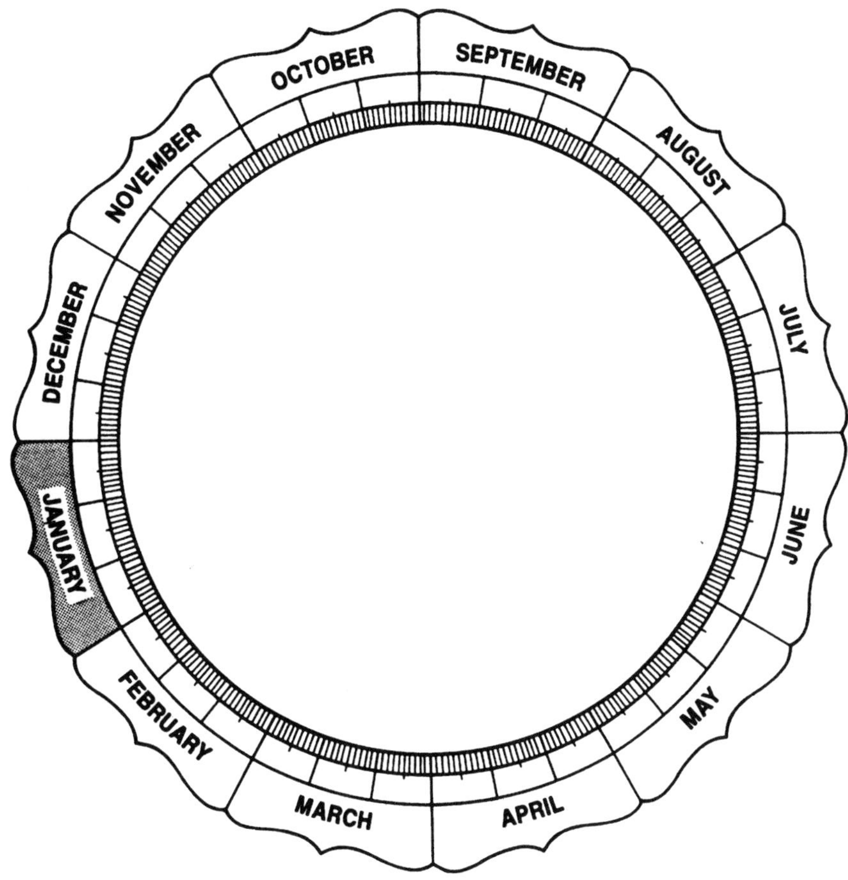

Figure 3 A circle chart for a person born in January

2

The Moon

POLICEMEN, hospital casualty workers and mental nurses are all aware that some people cannot handle the extra energy that is around at the time of a full Moon. The Moon exerts a strong influence on the tides, plants, animals – and us. Not everybody is jumpy or unhappy on a full Moon; some people are at their best at that time. The simplest way to work out what the Moon is doing is to go outside and look at it. Diaries, newspapers and almanacs also show the phases of the Moon. Figure 5 shows the phases of the Moon in detail, but if you are looking at the sky and you are not sure if the Moon is new or old, remember the word 'DOG', because the curve of the D is the shape of the new Moon and the G shape shows the old Moon! (If you prefer the word 'DOC' instead of 'DOG', then use that.)

New, full and quarter Moons at birth

If you can read an astrological ephemeris (the book of tables that astrologers use), you will soon be able to find the sign that the Moon occupied at the time of your birth. If you buy my book *Moon Signs*, you will find at the back a list of the positions of the Moon with full instructions for use. As soon as you have found your 'Moon sign', photocopy the chart on page 13, blocking out the Moon symbol. Write in your Sun sign next to the symbol for the Sun, which is on the left-hand side of the chart, and enter all the other zodiac signs in order in an *anti-clockwise* direction around the chart. Then enter the symbol for the Moon against the sign it was in at the time of your birth. The following instructions will show you whether the Moon

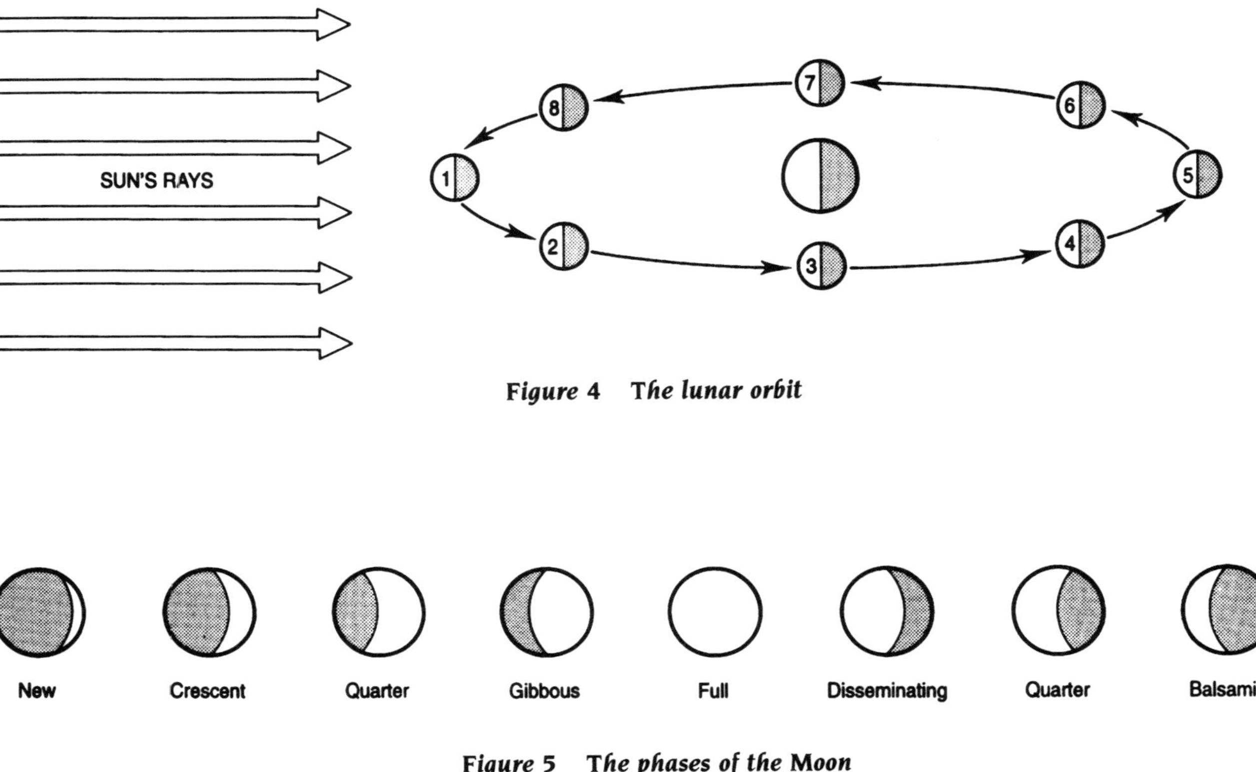

Figure 4 **The lunar orbit**

Figure 5 **The phases of the Moon**

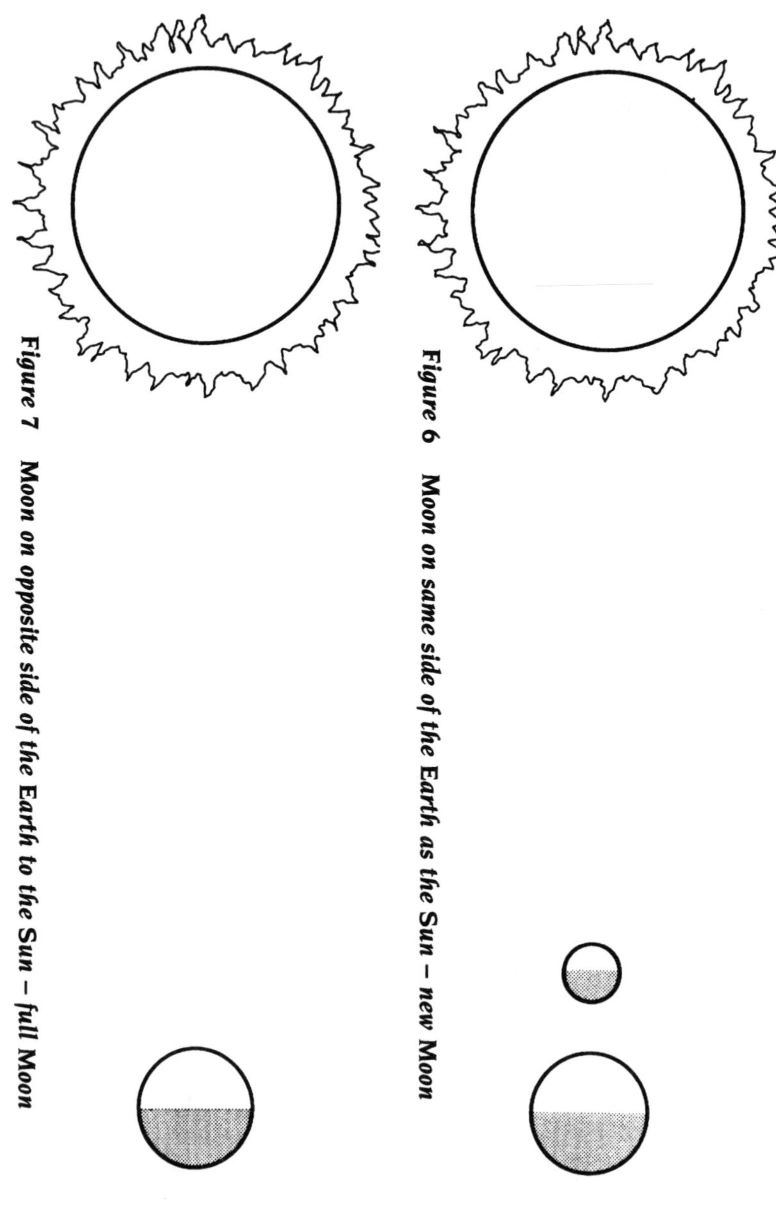

Figure 6 Moon on same side of the Earth as the Sun – new Moon

Figure 7 Moon on opposite side of the Earth to the Sun – full Moon

was new, full, quarter or whatever at the time of your birth. This has nothing to do with predictive astrology as such but it will get you into the habit of thinking in a circular – astrological – fashion.

On an astrologer's chart, the Moon moves much more swiftly than the Sun, therefore a new Moon is shown as a conjunction between the Sun and Moon. That is when they are both in the same place. A full Moon occurs when the Moon is opposite the Sun and the quarters obviously occur when the Moon is quarter way round the chart from the Sun.

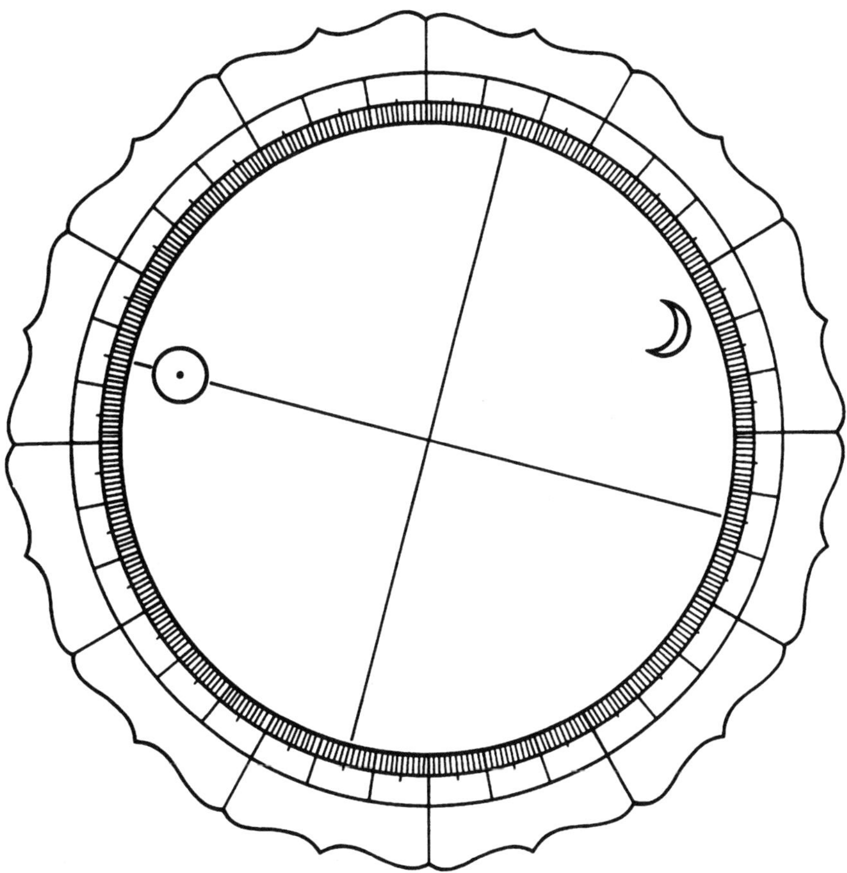

Figure 8 ***The full Moon is beginning to wane in this diagram***

If you keep an eye on your diary, the newspaper and the sky, you will soon be able to work out when the Moon returns to the same phase in which it was when you were born. A little observation over a period of months will show you whether this is a fortunate or an unfortunate monthly phase for you. Also note those times when you don't feel at your best or your happiest and see whether or not these times coincide with any particular phase of the Moon.

Eclipses

Eclipses usually occur in pairs and at about four- to five-month intervals. There can be as few as three and as many as six eclipses in a year. Normally, a solar eclipse is followed by a lunar eclipse a couple of weeks later, or vice versa. Some eclipses are easy to see in the sky, but most are partial and may not be visible in your part of the World. From an astrologer's point of view, the fact that an eclipse is partial or full shouldn't make much difference, but, like everyone else, we tend to take notice of the more spectacular ones. The Romans used to see these as portents of evil, and modern astrologers, for the most part, tend to agree with the Romans. Most eclipses pass ordinary people by without notice, which is just as well considering their frequency. However, if an eclipse falls on your Sun, Moon or ascendant (the point on your natal chart where night meets day), you will feel its effects strongly.

If you are far enough into astrology to understand a natal chart, you may like to consider the Ptolomeic theory of eclipses: an eclipse that occurs on a subject's ascendant can be felt three months afterwards. An eclipse on the nadir can be felt six months afterwards, while an eclipse on the descendant can be felt nine months afterwards. My own observation of eclipses is that, if one occurs on a subject's Sun, Moon or ascendant, they will feel it very powerfully within no more than a couple of days, and it will bring an unpleasant situation to a head. Eclipses that occur on other planets, angles, midpoints or other sensitive areas of the chart will also make themselves felt.

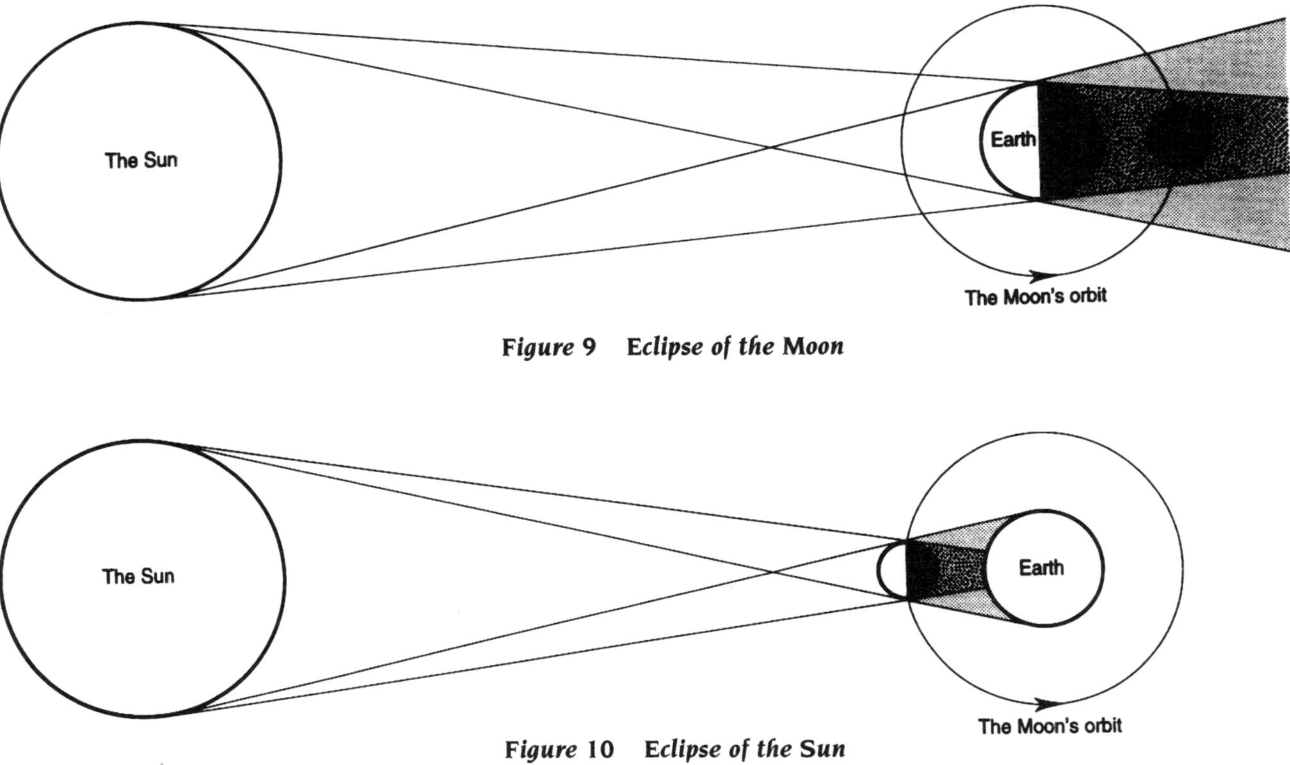

Figure 9 **Eclipse of the Moon**

Figure 10 **Eclipse of the Sun**

THE SAROS CYCLE

List of eclipses for the period 1995 to 2005

Type	*Date*	*Time*	*Position*
Lunar	15 April 1995	12.20	25 Libra
Solar	29 April 1995	17.36	08 Taurus
Lunar	8 Oct 1995	16.03	14 Aries
Solar	24 Oct 1995	04.28	00 Scorpio
Lunar	4 April 1996	00.12	14 Libra
Solar	17 April 1996	22.42	28 Aries
Lunar	27 Sept 1996	02.55	04 Aries
Solar	12 Oct 1996	13.59	19 Libra
Solar	9 March 1997	01.29	18 Pisces
Lunar	24 March 1997	04.40	03 Libra
Solar	2 Sept 1997	00.03	09 Virgo
Lunar	16 Sept 1997	18.47	23 Pisces
Solar	26 Feb 1998	17.30	07 Pisces
Lunar	13 March 1998	04.24	22 Virgo
Lunar	8 Aug 1998	02.26	15 Aquarius
Solar	22 Aug 1998	02.07	28 Leo
Lunar	6 Sept 1998	11.07	13 Pisces
Lunar	31 Jan 1999	16.21	11 Leo
Solar	16 Feb 1999	06.35	27 Aquarius
Lunar	28 July 1999	11.33	04 Aquarius
Solar	11 Aug 1999	11.04	18 Leo
Lunar	21 Jan 2000	04.46	00 Leo
Solar	5 Feb 2000	12.50	16 Aquarius
Solar	1 July 2000	19.36	10 Cancer
Lunar	16 July 2000	13.56	24 Capricorn
Solar	31 July 2000	02.13	08 Leo
Solar	25 Dec 2000	17.37	04 Capricorn
Lunar	9 Jan 2001	20.20	19 Cancer
Solar	21 June 2001	12.04	00 Cancer
Lunar	5 July 2001	14.58	13 Capricorn
Solar	14 Dec 2001	20.54	22 Sagittarius
Lunar	30 Dec 2001	10.28	08 Cancer
Lunar	26 May 2002	12.08	05 Sagittarius
Solar	10 June 2002	23.45	19 Gemini
Lunar	24 June 2002	21.28	03 Capricorn
Lunar	20 Nov 2002	01.44	27 Taurus
Solar	4 Dec 2002	07.33	11 Sagittarius

Type	*Date*	*Time*	*Position*
Lunar	16 May 2003	03.43	24 Scorpio
Solar	31 May 2003	04.09	09 Gemini
Lunar	9 Nov 2003	01.20	16 Taurus
Solar	23 Nov 2003	22.48	01 Sagittarius
Solar	10 April 2004	13.38	29 Aries
Lunar	4 May 2004	20.30	14 Scorpio
Solar	14 Oct 2004	02.56	21 Libra
Lunar	28 Oct 2004	03.04	05 Taurus
Solar	8 April 2005	20.42	19 Aries
Lunar	24 April 2005	09.57	04 Scorpio
Solar	3 Oct 2005	10.28	10 Libra
Lunar	17 Oct 2005	12.02	24 Aries

3

The Cycles of Time

PLEASE forgive me for calling the Sun and Moon planets when we all know that they aren't planets. All astrologers do this for the sake of simplicity and, anyway, *you* know what I mean!

Wherever the planets were when a subject was born, there are times when they return to the same place. Some of these planets move too quickly for this *planetary return* to be significant, while others move too slowly to return to their starting-point during the course of a human lifetime. However, even the slowest of them will move a sixth, a quarter, a third and, in most cases, half-way around the chart, sparking off events as they pass these tender spots on a subject's birthchart. By the way, you will be pleased to know that you don't have to own or understand a birthchart for this section of the book.

A brief introduction to the movements of the planets

The Moon moves around the Earth every 27.32 days, while the Sun's return is celebrated every year as a birthday. Mercury and Venus also land back at their starting-place roughly once a year, while Mars takes almost two years to get there. Jupiter takes about a year to work its way through each sign of the zodiac, and therefore returns to its natal position roughly every 12 years. Saturn makes its return approximately every 29.5 years. Uranus has an 84-year orbit and therefore makes a half-return after roughly 42 years, while Neptune, with its 165-year orbit, makes a half-return when the subject is around the age of 82. Pluto moves too slowly and in too eccentric an orbit to lay down any hard and fast rules about its aspects. The angles that a planet can make to its own natal position, or that any planet can make to any other, or to the ascendant or any other feature on a chart, are known as aspects. The major aspects are the conjunction, sextile, square, trine and opposition. (See page 24 for further explanation.) For technical reasons which I won't go into here, all these planets occasionally have slight variations in their orbits. Because the Earth and all the other planets orbit the Sun, there are times when we appear to be overtaking them. This apparent backwards motion of the planets is called retrograde motion. The Sun and the Moon never 'go retrograde'.

The planetary cycles

Just for your information or for future reference, here are the planetary orbits in list form:

The Earth orbits the Sun in approximately 365.25 days (one year).
The Moon orbits the Earth in 27.32 days.
Mercury orbits the Sun in 88 days.
Venus orbits the Sun in 225 days.
Mars orbits the Sun in 1 year, 10.5 months.
Jupiter orbits the Sun in 12 years.
Saturn orbits the Sun in 29 years.
Uranus orbits the Sun in 84 years.
Neptune orbits the Sun in 165 years.
Pluto orbits the Sun in 246 years.

There is absolutely no need for you to memorize these cycles, but there are a few that will become familiar. A point worth bearing in mind is that these cycles affect *everybody* and do not depend upon a specific birthchart. If you mix with other astrologers, you will soon become used to the terms 'the Saturn return' or the 'Uranus half-return'. So, this is what it all means.

The planetary movements in detail

The Moon ☽

The Moon travels around the Earth once each month. Therefore there will be one day in every 27.32 days when it returns to the place in which it was when a subject was born. This is called a *lunar return*. At this point in the book I suggest that you forget about the Moon, because apart from obvious things such as a woman having a menstrual period or one's credit card bills coming in, there shouldn't be too many earth-shattering things happening on a monthly basis. You will discover more about the technical side of lunar returns later on, in the more advanced chapters of this book.

The Earth ⊕

From an astrologer's point of view, the Earth stands still, and the Sun, the Moon and everything else moves around us. We know that this isn't the case at all, and that the spirit of Copernicus would be very upset to hear it. However, for the time being, let us assume that the Earth is the centre of the solar system.

The Sun ☉

From our perspective on Earth, the Sun appears to move through the whole zodiac once a year. A solar return is the time when the Sun returns to the place in which it was when a subject was born. We celebrate this annual return as a birthday, but there are some people whose solar return actually falls a day before or after their birthday. My own solar return usually occurs on 16 August, despite the fact that I was actually born just into 17 August. We have mixed feelings about birthdays, being both pleased to receive cards and gifts and also being a little peeved about getting older. These mixed feelings are typical of any planetary return. By the way, the phrase 'many happy returns of the day' comes from the astronomical and astrological phenomenon of the Solar return.

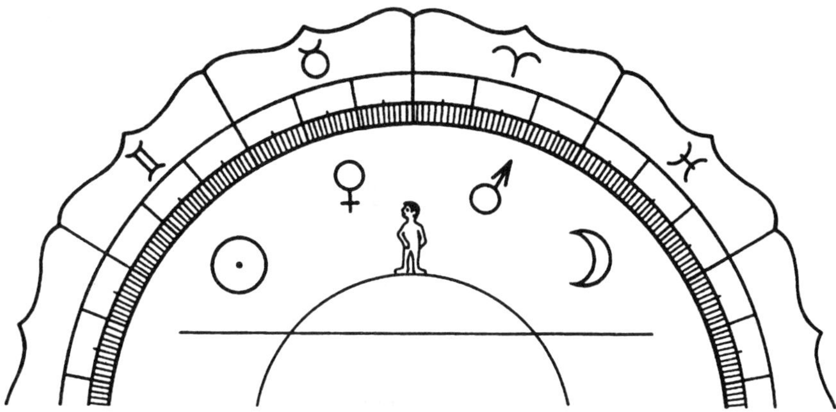

Figure 11 ***From our standpoint on the Earth, the planets appear to move around us***

Mercury ☿

Mercury moves very quickly and it is never far from the Sun. In common with all the other planets (except the Sun and Moon), there are times when it appears to be moving backwards! Mercury's return occurs once a year, around the time of a subject's birthday, and it makes the subject stop and think both about the year that has passed by and the one that is coming. Mercury is very much involved with all kinds of thinking. Unless you are far enough into astrology to understand a natal chart and to read the transits, don't worry about the exact day of the Mercury return, just accept that this is part and parcel of the rather introspective time around one's birthday.

Venus ♀

Venus moves less quickly than Mercury but it is never far from the Sun, and about once a year it will spend some time in retrograde motion. However, Venus usually returns to its own place at around the time of a subject's birthday. Venus's return will make a subject take some time to review their financial and relationship situation. It often sparks off a period of socializing, the desire for a holiday or to enjoy a bit of luxury.

Mars ♂

A Mars return occurs once every one year and 10.5 months, and is therefore a bit of a bore to work out by hand. If birthcharts are still uncharted territory for you, then don't worry about this section and skip over to Jupiter.

If you have reached the stage of understanding a birthchart, it is easy to look in your ephemeris to see when each Mars return occurs. This return will set off sudden and quite noticeable changes, but the outcome will depend upon the signs, houses and aspects that are involved. If, for instance, natal Mars is in the twelfth house, a return might bring a subject a great boost to their psychic powers, while simultaneously producing some kind of health setback due to this powerful return occurring *opposite* their sixth house of health. A Mars return in the first house will boost the subject's health, confidence and general life style, but it may have a murderous effect on their relationships (seventh house). Because Mars is one of the speedier of the planets, the effects of its returns, half-returns and other aspects should be over fairly quickly.

Jupiter ♃

Jupiter takes 12 years to make its return. If you understand natal charting, when trying to interpret this return you will need to take into account the sign and the house that natal Jupiter occupies as well as any planets that aspect Jupiter natally.

If you don't understand natal charting, then just remember that Jupiter is a bit of a double-edged sword. As you begin to read and learn about astrology, you will soon come to see Jupiter as 'the great benefic', or the planet that, along with Venus, bestows all kinds of good things upon its subjects. Alas, this is not quite the case. You may remember reading that the old Roman god Jupiter (or Jove, if you prefer) tossed down thunderbolts from Mount Olympus whenever he was out of sorts. Therefore a Jupiter return can bring some sudden and unpleasant changes into a subject's life, but the odd thing is that in the long run there is usually something beneficial that comes out of these unpleasant events. If the subject loses something or someone from their life under a Jupiter return, it is probably no bad thing.

It is not difficult to work out that any subject is likely to experience Jupiter returns at the ages of 12, 24, 36, 48, 60, 72, 84 and 96. These do tend to be *lucky* years, when nice things happen to us all. At these times, a subject can expect to form good friendships with people who share the same beliefs and outlook on life. They may start a career, find a mate, make a home, give life to a child or find their feet in some way at these times. Greater confidence in themselves and in their deeply felt hopes, wishes and beliefs will carry them through any problems that may arise.

It is also not difficult to see that the Jupiter half-returns occur at the ages of 6, 18, 30, 42, 54, 66, 78, 80 and 92. These can be times of setback and loss, but, because Jupiter is *basically* one of the planetary 'goodies', this is likely to be really devastating only if other, more important, planetary events are occurring at the same time.

Saturn ♄

This is the planet that all astrologers mutter about darkly, because the Saturn returns at the ages of 29/30 and 57/59 can take a lot of living through. Oddly enough, these hard times can ultimately bring great benefits in their wake, because they set up lessons and challenges which, when grasped, bring terrific rewards. The easiest way to understand Saturn's effects is to see them in the form of a list. Bear in mind that planets waver in their orbits, so, until you can study each chart in detail, the dates may be a little out of true.

Some help with the terminology

If you remember that astrologers see the signs of the zodiac in terms of a circle around the Earth, the following expressions become easy to understand. When a planet goes around the zodiac and lands back where it started, this is known as a *return*. Therefore, in the list below, the *Saturn return* shows those ages when Saturn orbits the Sun (and also all the signs of the zodiac that we see from our standpoint on the Earth) and lands back where it started.

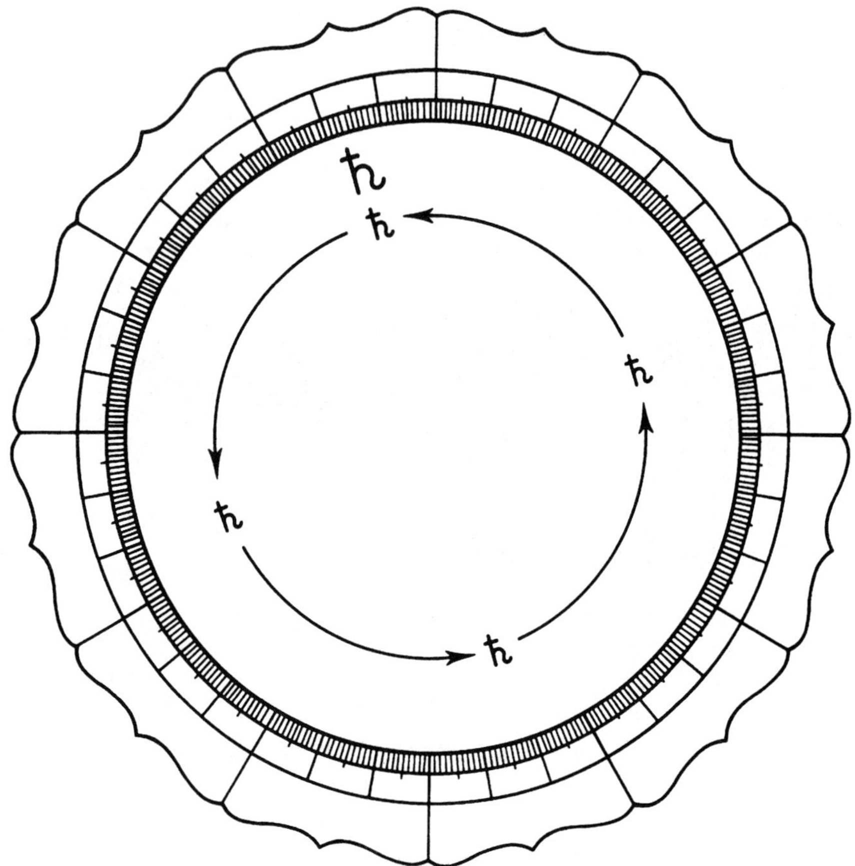

Figure 12 The Transits of Saturn
The Saturn return, half- and quarter-returns

When any planet is in the same place as any other, this is called a *conjunction*. A *square* aspect is when a planet is three signs away around the zodiac circle. When looking at an astrological chart, this would be a quarter of the way round the chart, or 90 degrees away. An *opposition* is six signs away, or 180 degrees away if you prefer. If you are looking at a planet that is half way around the zodiac, and therefore opposite to its natal placement, this is usually called a half-return.

THE TRANSITS OF SATURN

Age	*Aspect*	*Probable effects*
7/8	Square	Sadness, loss, realization that life is not all fun and games.
14/15	Opposition	Responsibilities begin to weigh heavily; possible family problems.
22/23	Square	Often a good time, although extra responsibility is often sought and there may be disappointments.
29/30	Return	Taking responsibility for one's own life; realizing what one really wants to do and to be.
37/38	Square	Not usually a bad time, although extra work challenges or other responsibilities may be sought. Women may realize that the biological clock is ticking away too quickly.
44/45	Opposition	Middle age, with all that that implies; end of childbearing and of some career possibilities. Health may become less reliable.
52/53	Square	This may or may not be a bad time, although the last real thrust towards major work ambitions can be made at this time.
57/59	Return	Often a time of great change. Health may be an issue but reverses in business or personal life are not uncommon at this time. Can be good if challenges are accepted. May be a realization that something needs to be changed or even left behind for good.

The nicer Saturn aspects, such as the trines and sextiles, are best left until you get further into astrology because they vary in their timing and may not occur at the times that I suggest.

Uranus ♅

The orbit of Uranus is 84 years, but variations during that orbit can alter the time of the all-important half-return. Uranus is going through a speeding-up process at the moment, so those who are now approaching their forties will experience the half-return at the age of 39. Older subjects will have experienced this at 40, 41 or even 42. Uranus, the 'breakout' planet, brings issues of freedom and originality to the fore, so, if a subject has been living a very conventional life up to the time of the return, they may kick over the traces when it comes. The outcome of this will vary according to the sign and house in which Uranus is at birth. It will also be modified by any other planetary aspects that may be involved. From now on, whenever you read your newspaper, make a mental note of the ages of those who suddenly lose their cool and run off with someone totally unsuitable, walk out of their jobs to become pop singers, or shoot a neighbour's noisy dog! The chances are that whatever has been driving them to distraction over the years comes to the fore in a dramatic way on the good old 'Uranus half'.

Oddly enough, astrologers don't seem to take much notice of the Uranus squares that occur at 21 and 63, but these also force a subject to reappraise their life and to make what appear to be sudden and unexpected changes. Astrological theory tells us that squares are challenging, difficult and altogether uncomfortable things to have. In fact, since doing the research on this book, I am rapidly coming to the conclusion that they are not all that bad. They seem to mark the times when we make decisions based on what has gone before and what we want from the future.

All these so-called outer planets have fairly eccentric orbits, so it is worth looking only at the aspects that they make in any detail against a proper birthchart.

N.B. The Sun, Moon, Mercury, Venus and Mars are called *inner planets* while Jupiter, Saturn, Uranus, Neptune and Pluto are called *outer planets*.

Neptune ♆

If Neptune's orbit was totally regular, with no retrograde motion, and no apparent speeding up or slowing down occurring at perihelion (closest to the Sun) and apogee (furthest from the Sun), one could plot the exact timing of its various aspects. However, for the current generation, the good times should occur at around the age of 28 and 52, while the worst times should be at around 42 and 83 – give or take a year or two either way. The best aspects of Neptune bring love, unconditional friendship, spiritual happiness, an outburst of artistic or creative talent and an appreciation of the finer things of life. The bad times may bring sadness, strange health problems, confusion and a loss of faith in everything.

Pluto ♇

Pluto's orbit is so eccentric that it has to be looked at against each individual birthchart. However, those who are approaching early middle age now will feel the effects of the Pluto square at any time from their late thirties to their early forties.

So, as you can see, that sensitive point from around the age of 39 to around the age of 42 can be very difficult, because all the planets seem to be conspiring to bring changes and uncontrolled events. If you who are reading this are already older than this, count yourself lucky!

Chiron ⚷

Chiron is a planetoid or large asteroid which is being given attention now due to the fact that modern astrology computer programs allow us to track its orbit. Chiron is known as the *wounded healer* and it is said to be concerned with physical and emotional pain. The mythology behind Chiron may help you to understand its nature.

Chiron was the King of the Centaurs and the teacher of heroes, including Hercules, Jason and Perseus. He was accidentally shot in the heel by one of Hercules's poisoned arrows and the wound festered. Chiron couldn't be cured but, being immortal, he couldn't die either, so he suffered terribly. Meanwhile, Uranus was also not particularly happy, being tied to a rock in the sea while birds were pecking at his liver. Hercules freed Uranus but this act cost Uranus his immortality. When Uranus asked Jupiter to give it back, Jupiter couldn't help unless he found someone who would swap his own immortality for mortality. Chiron agreed to do this so that he could end his suffering and die. Chiron went on to take his place in the heavens as the constellation Centaurus. Before his accident, Chiron was known as the greatest of the healers and his daughter Manta was said to have invented the mantic arts, such as crystalmancy, chriomancy etc. The association of Chiron with the Centaurs has prompted some astrologers to link this planetoid to the sign of Sagittarius. Others, including myself, link him to Virgo because of his association with health and teaching. Try looking at the position of Chiron in natal, progressed and transit charts for evidence of suffering.

More terminology explained

The ascendant (or asc.)

This is the point on the eastern horizon where day meets night and where the horizon bisects the ecliptic (the path of the Sun). It represents the subject's starting point in life and may give a clue as to his early experiences. It may account for the subject's appearance and his health and wellbeing. The ascendant can considerably modify the Sun sign. Planets that are close to the ascendant have a strong influence. Progressions and transits over the ascendant spark off times of change and new beginnings of various kinds.

The descendant (or dsc.)

The sign on the descendant gives a clue about the kind of relationships the subject seeks and the type of people he draws to him. Progressions and transits across the descendant bring beginnings and endings in connection with relationships, business partnerships, friendships and other close associations.

The midheaven (or MC – medium coeli)

The sign on the midheaven represents the subject's direction in life and gives a clue about his ambitions and goals. Progressions and transits to this point bring beginnings and endings in connection with a subject's aims and aspirations. Job changes or changes of pace can occur at such times.

The nadir (or IC – immum coeli or lower-midheaven)

The sign on the nadir denotes the manner in which the subject's life starts and ends. It also refers to his background, family history and his family and domestic circumstances throughout life. Progressions and transits here will bring changes in connection with property, premises and family life.

The vertex (plural – vertices)

The vertex is a little beyond the scope of this book. Indeed, it is something that I myself am only beginning to seriously investigate now. It is supposed to be the most westerly point of the planets on a birthchart. It appears to be a very sensitive point regarding our relationships with others. The vertex shows the emotions that we experience through our relationships with others and the lessons that these teach us. The vertex seems to show our most vulnerable and sensitive inner needs and thus, where other people can hurt us most. If you are into natal charting and you have a computer program that shows you the vertex, take a look through a few charts and examine the sign, house and any aspects to the vertex. It should be used when examining partnerships and it is the aspects from another person's Sun, ascendant and midheaven to a subject's vertex that have the most impact. The most important aspects between the two charts are considered to be the conjunction and opposition.

From a predictive point of view, planets that make progressions or transits to the vertex have a profound effect on partnership matters. It may be helpful for me to tell you about the time when Uranus spent some time travelling backwards and forwards over my vertex. In 1977 my husband was extremely ill with a heart condition which was eventually cured by a quadruple bypass operation. As my husband's Sun happens to be a degree and a half away from my vertex, Uranus also was crossing back and forth over his Sun at this time.

The part of fortune

This is one of the many Arabic parts and is also really beyond the scope of this book. The part of fortune shows where and how the subject will gain honours, make money or be lucky during his life. Progressions and transits to the part of fortune should bring opportunities for gain. I experienced a great boost to my career during 1989 and 1990 when Saturn, Uranus and Neptune crossed my part of fortune.

Ages of change

The following list will make it easy to spot the major times of change in everyone's life. Remember that the planets move at a slightly different rate for different age groups, so be a little flexible when interpreting the years. Only the slower-moving outer planets are used for this table.

Age	*Planetary movement*
7	Saturn square natal Saturn
12	Jupiter return
14	Saturn opposition natal Saturn (Saturn half-return)
18	Jupiter opposition natal Jupiter (Jupiter half-return)
21	Saturn square natal Saturn
24	Jupiter return
29/30	Saturn return
30	Jupiter opposition natal Jupiter
36	Saturn square natal Saturn; Jupiter return
39/40ish	Uranus opposition natal Uranus (Uranus half-return)
42	Neptune square natal Neptune; Jupiter opposition natal Jupiter
44	Saturn opposite natal Saturn
48	Jupiter return
51	Saturn square natal Saturn
52	Neptune trine natal Neptune
57/59	Saturn return
60	Jupiter return

63	Uranus square natal Uranus
66	Saturn square natal Saturn
72	Jupiter return
75	Saturn opposition natal Saturn
80	Saturn square natal Saturn
80ish	Uranus return
84	Jupiter return

4

Natal Charting

YOU WILL have come across the terms *natal chart* and *birthchart* at various times in this book, and before we move on any further we ought to take a very brief look at this. A natal chart is a map of the heavens at the moment of the birth of a subject, an enterprise, a country or anything else that comes into manifestation. The very word *horoscope* means 'map of the hour'. The natal chart describes the character of the person or enterprise in question.

Information

There are many books on every aspect of natal charting and many, many courses that are available to students. Nowadays, computers take all the sweat out of the figure work, but it is still advisable to learn how to do this by hand in the first place, so that you know how the figures are arrived at. The good news is that none of this is difficult, and the maths involved are only addition and subtraction. Computers and their programs are getting cheaper all the time, and there is plenty of information and many people around to help you. Any magazine on the subject of astrology and related matters will carry advertisements for books, schools, groups and courses galore. There is information elsewhere in this book that should help you find answers to your questions.

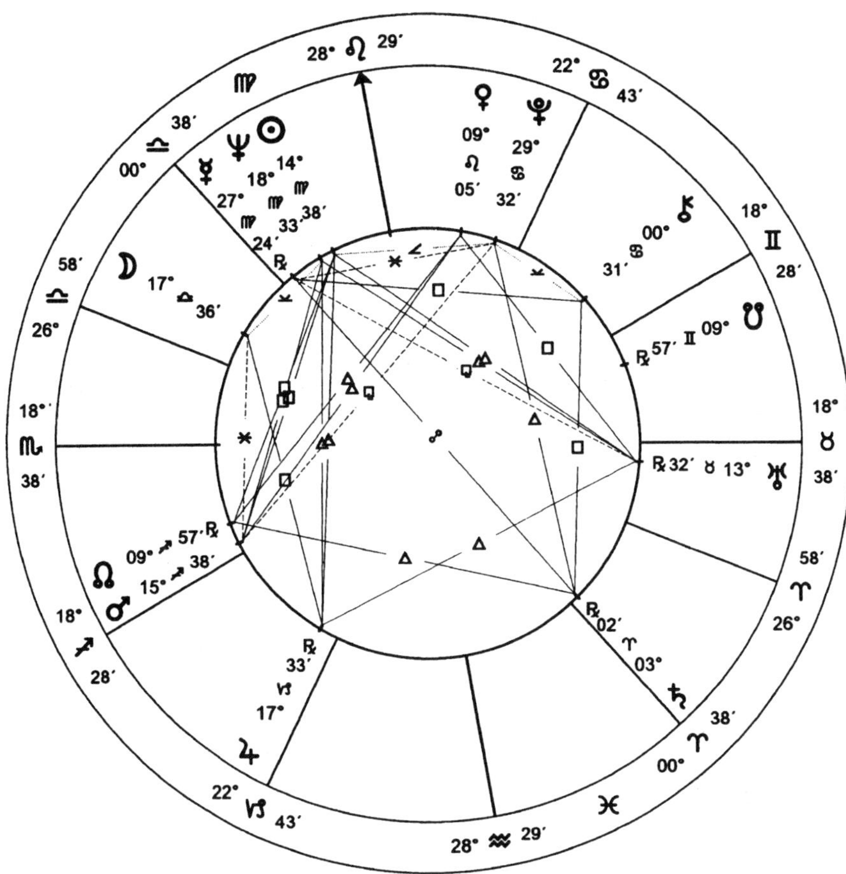

Figure 13 A Natal Chart
The zodiac signs are in the outer ring, the inner ring shows the planets in the houses, and the inner circle shows the aspects

Martin Davis
Natal Chart
Sep 7 1937
10:58 CST +6:00
Saint Louis, MO, USA
38N37 090W12

Predictive work

You really do need to be able to draw up and interpret a natal chart, even if you have to look up some of the meanings of the planets and the aspects before you can get the best out of some of the predictive techniques that follow in this book. However, even if you can erect only half a chart, by placing the planets around a circle and forgetting the ascendant and midheaven, you will find the transits to these planets pretty easy to work out and interpret with the aid of a good book or two. It doesn't take long for a student to see that when Saturn moves opposite their Moon they are likely to become depressed, or that when Jupiter makes a good angle to their Venus they are likely to be lucky and happy.

5

The Next Step

UP TO NOW, we have been looking at techniques that don't require any real astrological know-how at all, but from this point onwards you really do need to be able to put together and understand a birthchart. For those of you who are beginning to get into *real* astrology, here is a recap on birthcharts or, as astrologers call them, natal charts.

Where to find information

Firstly, you can learn natal charting or, indeed, any other form of astrology from books, correspondence courses, evening classes or short vacation courses, or from somebody who is either running classes from their home or who is willing to show you the basics for a fee. I taught myself, and my starting-point was a book that is now called *Parkers' Astrology*, by Derek and Julia Parker. It was called something else then and it wasn't as good as it is now, so I expect that a few thousand other astrologers have also learned their astrology from this book.

Whatever standard you have reached in your astrology and whatever country you live in, you will find it very helpful to arm yourself with the excellent book that is put out each year by the Urania Trust in London, and which is issued free of charge each year to anyone who requests it (see further reading section). My current copy is called *Astrology 1994: the free guide to astrology world-wide*. It covers schools, postal courses, local groups, meetings and journals of all kinds all over the world. It also advertises computer companies that specialize in astrological software, bookshops, mail-order houses, publishers, international events, conferences and just about everything there is to help you find information, like-minded people and organizations of every possible description. Many bookshops and all publishers will send out book lists and most will be happy to send you books by post.

Where to begin

Before you consider doing any kind of serious predictive work, you must be able to put together a natal chart and interpret it. As soon as you can do this reasonably proficiently, you can seriously think about moving on to predictive work. The good news is that natal charting is not difficult. In addition to this, most people begin to pick up the simplest form of predictive techniques quite naturally while learning natal charting. If you have no astrological knowledge at all, I suggest that you hang on to this book until you have passed this hurdle. A further point is that you cannot fail to become absolutely fascinated by natal interpretation, so it is definitely not to be thought of as some kind of penance that has to be paid before getting to the interesting stuff.

A recap on natal charting

A natal chart, often known as a birthchart, tells an astrologer all about the *character* of their client. This is a picture of the sky at the moment of a person's birth and it is set for the date, time and place of his or her birth. The starting-point of any natal chart is the ascendant. This is the point directly to the left of the chart (where nine o'clock would be on a clock face). The ascendant gives the astrologer a good deal of information on the childhood and background of their subject and also of the early programming that went on in their life. The 12 astrological *houses* are marked around in an *anti-clockwise* direction from the ascendant. These houses can be of equal size, or they can be arranged in ways that reflect the shape of the earth and are therefore unequal in size. There are many methods in use, but if you are just getting into astrology stick to the equal house method. You may never bother with any of the other methods, but, if you decide to have a go, try either the Placidus or the

Koch systems and see how you like them.

The signs that the Sun, Moon and planets occupy all show how these heavenly bodies influence our nature, while the houses reveal how these planets are put to use. For instance, a subject who has Mercury (the planet that rules his ability to think) in the sixth house in Aquarius would be quick, clever and rather detached in their approach (Aquarius). They would use their mind for some form of analytical work and they would be happy in a world of contracts, figure-work and details. They may be a bit short on sympathy and the ability to empathize with others, because their mind would be cool and scientific and their tongue quick and sarcastic. Mercury in Cancer in the twelfth house would belong to someone whose thinking processes were diametrically opposite to the person with the previous placement, that is, kindly, sympathetic, emotional and, oddly enough, rather businesslike.

I can't go into natal charting in any depth in this book, but, just as a reminder to those of you who are moving into *real* astrology, here are the steps that you will need to take.

1. *Either* buy a computer program that will work out the figures for a natal chart, progress it, produce a list of transits and put everything together in chart form, and then teach yourself to use this. *Or* teach yourself how to do it by hand. If you are serious about astrology, do both!
2. If you are going to work out a chart by hand, take the following steps. Find the date of your subject's birth in an ephemeris and list the planetary positions. Adjust those planets from the time given in the ephemeris to the time of birth, concentrating especially on the faster moving planets and the Moon.
3. Now you will need to find the ascendant. The following extract, taken from my book *Rising Signs*, shows the method of erecting a natal chart for my daughter Helen, who was born in London, England. If you decide to try the method for yourself, do it first and then check thc computer chart on page 40 to see how close you managed to get. If you want to make calculations for births away from the magic Greenwich line of meridian, you will need to use my book *Understanding Astrology*, Derek and Julia Parker's *Parker's*

Astrology or some other book that specializes in natal charting.

Calculating your ascendant by hand

It is worth noting here that astrology is a creative and interpretive skill which suits the slightly arty or linguistic type of person, therefore the person who makes a good natural astrologer is usually a poor mathematician. I am an absolute dunce where maths are concerned, yet I can calculate an ascendant, which goes to show that anyone can.

Here is the chart for my daughter Helen. She was born in London at 2.18 (2.18 am) on 21 August 1965. (NB: I have used a *midnight* ephemeris for these calculations.)

1. As Helen was born in London, there is no need to make any adjustment for place of birth. Astrological calculations are based on the proximity of the birth to the Greenwich meridian.

   02.18.00
   1.00.00 –
   01.18.00

2. An August birth means that British Summer Time was in operation, therefore deduct one hour making the birth time 01.18 GMT.

3. The sidereal time (exact star time rather than calendar time) at midnight on 21 August was 21 hours 56 minutes 25 seconds.

   21.56.25

4. Add the time of birth to the sidereal time. Remember that when adding there are 60 seconds to a minute and 60 minutes to an hour.

   21.56.25
   1.18.00 +
   23.14.25

5. Now you will have to make an extra calculation which is called 'interval time'. This means that you add 10 seconds for every hour, 5 for every half hour and 3 for every 20 minutes. If you forget this, the chart will be slightly

   23.14.25
   13 +
   23.14.38

inaccurate but not by so much that the actual rising sign will be changed.

6. Now look up the resulting figures in ephemeris (book of ascendants and planetary positions).
7. In Helen's case, when we look in the ephemeris, we can see that her figure of 23hrs 14 mins 38 secs falls between 23.12.10 which comes out as 17° 37′ of Cancer and 23.15.52 which comes out as 18° 20′ of Cancer. For most purposes the round figure of 18° of Cancer which falls between the two will be quite good enough.

23.12.10
=17°37′

23.15.52
=18°20′
=Approx. 18°

4. Mark the ascendant/descendant line on an astrological chart and then divide into 12 equal houses. Arrange the 12 zodiac signs from the ascendant onwards. Mark in the midheaven and the nadir.
5. Finally place all the planets and any other features that you want to use in their correct slots in the chart.
6. Start to interpret the chart by looking up the meaning of the ascendant, the Sun, the Moon, the planets and anything else on which you can find information.

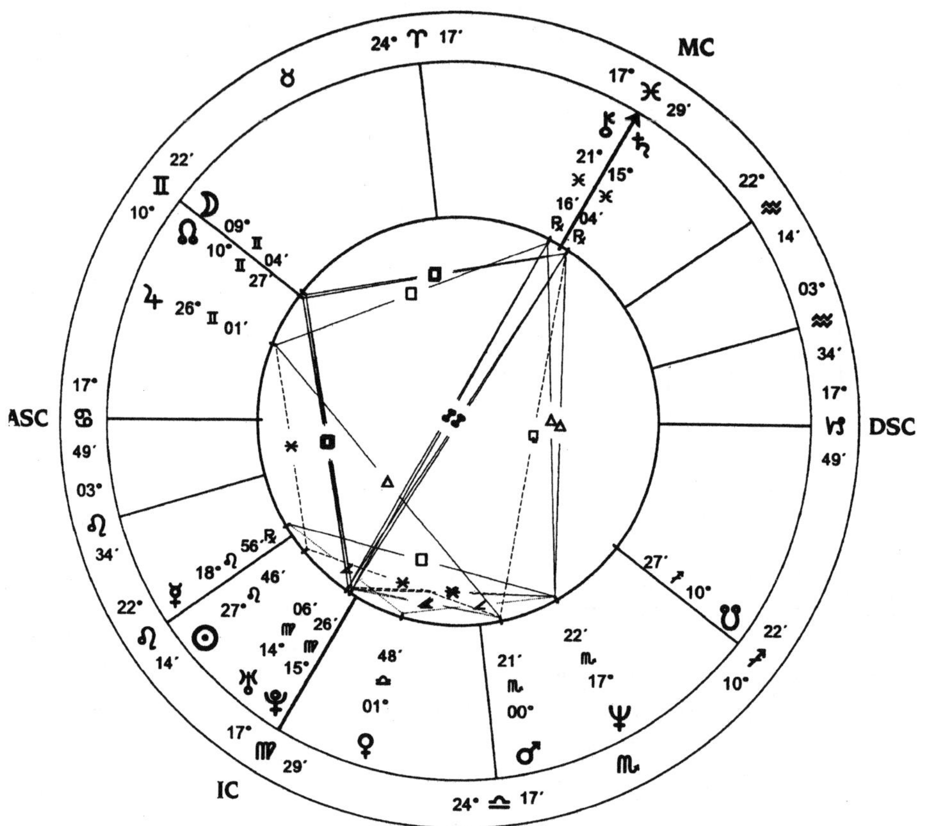

Figure 14 Helen's natal chart

Helen Fenton
Natal Chart
Aug 21 1965
02:18 BST -1:00
Carshalton, England
51N22 000W10

KEY
ASC = Ascendant
DSC = Descendant
MC = Midheaven
IC = Nadir

6

Computers, Programs and other Nightmares

My personal experiences with computers

DURING the 1960s and 1970s I augmented the family income by doing a variety of temporary and part-time jobs. Somewhere along the line I began to add the occasional astrology, palmistry or tarot reading to my repertoire. The fact that these skills eventually made my fortune took me as much by surprise as it did everyone else. By the early 1980s I had turned the back room of our house into an office and consulting room, and it soon became imperative that I find the quickest and most accurate way of giving clients the information they needed. Tarot and palmistry played their part, but I was always most fascinated by astrology.

In the late 1970s I met a young astrologer who worked out his astrological figures by means of a strange collection of metal boxes that made up a primitive 'PET' computer. At about the same time I was getting to grips with the early forms of word processor and computerized telex machines, so the potential of this kind of technology for astrology was already obvious to me. Unfortunately, the cost of the PET equipment and the American Matrix astrology program was way out of my pocket and I had to wait until affordable British software and hardware became available. Some time later, my son Stuart (then a scruffy schoolboy) began to get interested in computers, and he talked me into buying a battered second-hand Dragon. Needless to say, after playing around on this for a few weeks, he left it to collect dust in my office. I discovered a firm called Astrocalc who supplied a simple program that worked on a portable tape recorder plugged into the back of the Dragon, and for the first time I was able to generate the figures for a natal and a progressed chart at the touch of a few buttons.

Commercially speaking, it was still much quicker and easier for me to draw up my charts by hand. I was pretty nifty in doing hand charts by then, while it took time to set up and encourage the temperamental Dragon. Longitude and latitude had to be found and entered, and the natal and progressed figures read off from the screen (no printer in those days) and put onto a hand-drawn chart. However, the Dragon was useful for checking a particularly awkward chart, and it confirmed my feeling that this was the way forward. By the mid-1980s I was earning enough money from my books to invest in a decent computer and dot-matrix printer which I kept solely for astrology. Many computers have come and gone in my office over the years and they will doubtless continue to do so.

Hardware, or which computer should you buy?

Until recently, astrology programs didn't require terribly sophisticated computers, and practically anything that was available would do the job. This situation has changed over the last couple of years, and, while it is still possible to buy a very basic program, if you want anything other than the simplest information you will need to consider buying something decent. There is some software that will run on an Apple Macintosh and some that can be found for Omega and Atari machines, but most is suitable only for the IBM clones and, increasingly, for use with Windows. Modern high-quality colour screens produce wonderful charts, and these can be printed out in colour if that is what you want.

In the simplest terms, if you have access to any kind of computer, use the one you've got and find a program that will work on it. If you wish to buy a new machine, think about *all* the things you and your family are likely to use it for (accounts, games, etc.) and buy something suitable. I know a number of people who have got off the ground by buying second-hand machines from friends who are upgrading. Computer consultant Roy Gillett doesn't recommend this due to the expense, the lack of help and the cost of repairs if the machine breaks down. It is now possible to buy a 486 SX machine that will handle MS DOS and the Windows programs at a very reasonable price, with a warranty and backup available for dealing with problems.

My current machine is a Gateway 486DX-33 with Hewlett Packard Laserjet 4L laser printer. I currently use the Solar Fire program for most of my astrology work. I also run Chartwheels II (on MS DOS) on an 80-megabyte portable computer, and it works well, except for the fact that it is rather slow and that the screen is not coloured. I have recently bought a Dell Latitude 50 laptop, which is about the best machine on the market for any purpose at the time of writing. I use Solar Fire on the machine. I have bought all the Matrix programs for this machine and shall shortly have them installed on my Gateway too.

Every year I seem to replace either a computer, or printer or a program. These are the tools of my trade, and when something wears out I replace it with something that is bigger, better and faster.

Printers

Practically any printer will cope with astrology, though the old 'daisy-wheel' printers that were suitable only for word processing are no good. I wouldn't recommend the tiny Canon portable printer either. Any kind of dot-matrix, laser, bubble-jet or anything else that can cope with graphics will work, but, obviously, the better the quality of printer, the better the appearance of the printed-out material. At the moment, black and white printing is good enough for most astrologers, but in years to come I expect that colour printing will become the norm. Quite a few reasonably priced colour ink-jet and dot-matrix printers are now available. However, other people tell me that the toner for these is very expensive and apt to run out fairly quickly. I expect the technology for this will soon become cheaper and more efficient. Astrology apart, if you have other uses for a colour printer, then you will need to look into this for yourself.

Software, the washing machine factor

Some years ago, washing machines began to be produced in more and more sophisticated forms, with a tremendous variety of washing programs for every kind of garment. The upshot of all this is that most of us only ever use two or maybe three of the programs: cool, medium or hot. Who wants to run a machine on a special program just for the one awkward garment that needs it? It is quicker to wash out that tricky silk blouse by hand! Much the same goes for computers and astrology programs. If you want to make astrology your life's work and to know all there is about every aspect of it, buy a 486 machine at the very least and also invest in a top of the range program.

Astrology is my job, and I would be daft not to keep up with the latest equipment, but if it were just a hobby or a means of earning pin money, I wouldn't go to the trouble and expense that I do now. Therefore, if you only want to be able to *use* the darned thing to produce a few different kinds of charts, go for something simple and, over a period of time, work your way up the ladder until you have all that you need. It usually costs very little to upgrade existing software. It is a good idea to visit people and places where computerized astrology is being demonstrated and to ask for advice from those who already use such programs. However, astrologers can be very dedicated to their own favourite programs and there may be something else on the market that is more suitable for your needs, so read the brochures, talk to people and look around before buying.

Software 'toys'

Nowadays, there are some extremely inexpensive programs advertised in ordinary computer magazines, and these are aimed at people who are interested in astrology as a hobby. I recently experimented with one called Visions and it took me back to the old days of the Dragon, because it produces an excellent list of natal data but a pretty useless chartwheel. Visions runs on Windows, it is very easy to install and dead easy to use. It offers a natal chart and a natal data list and it also gives the transits for one particular day. Visions includes a written report on a subject's character and a written forecast for the chosen day. This program may be limited but it has one absolutely terrific feature, and that is the Gazetteer. As with many other programs, you can enter the name of the birth town in order to find the latitude and longitude. However, Visions displays maps of the world, so all the operator has to do is to click the mouse on the place of birth and, bingo, up come the coordinates! Wonderful! The poor quality of the chartwheel makes this pretty useless for a professional astrologer, but it is great fun and, at roughly the cost of a good pair of shoes, this program beats hand-working a chart into a cocked hat! There may be other 'hobby' programs that can handle progressions, aspects and transits for a period of time (rather than for one day), but I haven't used them. The message here is to look around and see what is available before buying anything and, even then, accept the fact that you may make some kind of mistake. For this reason, if nothing else, it would be better to use a pukka astrology software firm where you can get advice and also exchange and update programs as and when you discover exactly what you want.

It is possible to be an astrologer without using computers at all. After all, I managed to do this for ten years before getting computerized. But computers do remove the effort from even the most basic of astrological tasks, they are accurate and they encourage astrologers to try things that are simply not possible to do by hand.

Part Two

The Techniques of Prediction

7

Transits

THE FIRST PART of this book was written with beginners in mind – or even for those of you who have little or no real astrological knowledge at all. You may have already spotted the fact that Chapter 3, *The Cycles of Time*, concentrated on transits, although there you didn't need to be able to make up even the simplest form of chart. From this point on, you will need to be able to put together a simple natal chart and to read an ephemeris. Even if you cannot work out an ascendant, you will still be able to get something from the chapters on transits and solar arc progressions. However, if you can happily erect and interpret a natal chart, and understand the energies of the planets, aspects, angles and other sensitive points that are in those charts, you will get much more out of the remainder of this book.

If you take a look at the sky just before dawn on a cloudless morning, you will notice two or three stars that seem to hang about after the others have gone. Alternatively, wait for a cloudless night just after the Sun has set, and you will notice two or three stars glittering brightly in the dark blue heavens. These 'stars' are actually planets, and the chances are that, if you look towards the area where the Sun is rising or setting, you will spot bright and beautiful Venus and the smaller and duller Mercury. Elsewhere in the sky, depending upon the time of year, you may find another very bright planet, Jupiter, and perhaps the smaller and slightly reddish Mars or the similarly small but slightly yellowish Saturn. You will need an astronomer's telescope to see Uranus, Neptune or Pluto.

The reason that I begin this chapter by suggesting that you actually take a *look* at the sky is to remind student astrologers

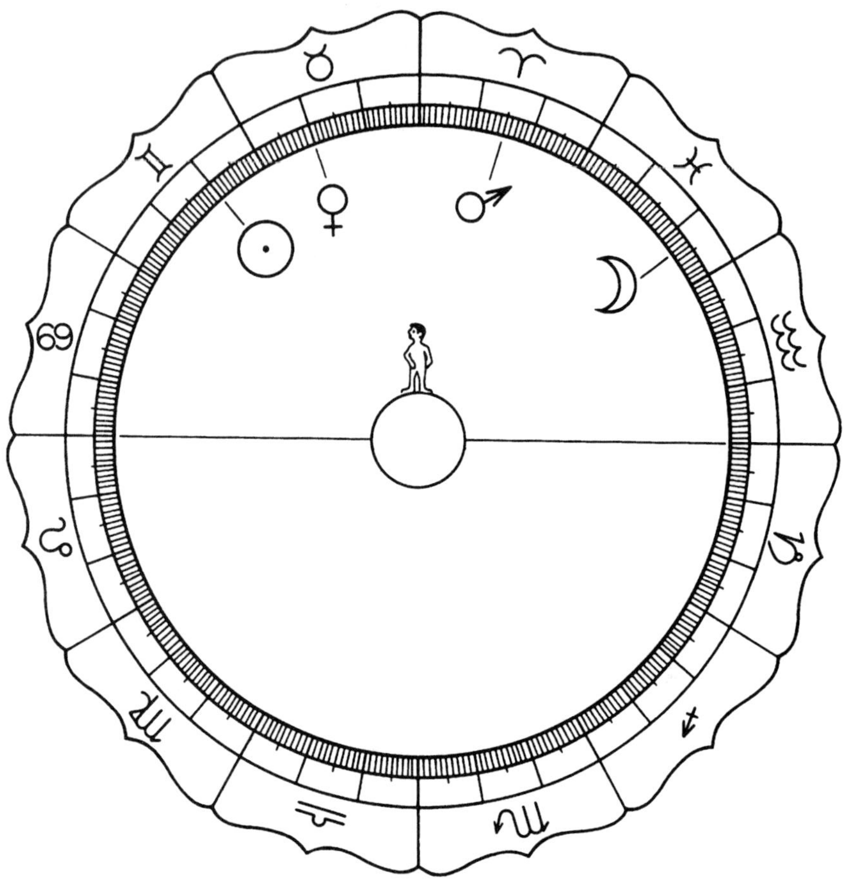

Figure 15 ***Try looking at the sky from time to time, if only to see what the Moon is doing***

that the planets don't just exist in the pages of your ephemeris or in the workings of your computer, but that they are very clearly there, in the heavens, working their magic on us at every twist and turn of their orbits. The second reason for my suggesting this is that all forms of 'progression' rely upon mathematical adjustments of a natal chart, while the transiting planets are literally right there in the sky, affecting you, me and everything on Earth.

My apologies for stating the obvious, but when you have found the transits that you want to look at, check them out against the natal chart and also the progressed one if you wish.

Getting down to work

Now turn back to your ephemeris or your computer and make a list of today's transits. The following extract (figure 16) is from the *World Ephemeris for the 20th Century – 1900 to 2000 at Midnight*, which is freely available from every astrological book dealer. If you have a different ephemeris, don't worry; they are all more or less the same. I like this one because the print is a little larger than in some of the others. I also suggest that you use a *midnight* ephemeris rather than a noon one, but this is a matter of personal preference. Unfortunately, today's astrologers will soon also need to buy an ephemeris for the 21st century.

Sadly, my favourite ephemeris does not give the position of Chiron, so I also keep a copy of *The American Ephemeris for the 20th Century* handy for this (see figure 17).

If you only want to look at the transits for some time during the current year, then you will probably have a copy of *Raphael's Astronomical Ephemeris* handy. This gives all the planetary positions (with the exception of Chiron) as well as many other astrological details for one particular year (see figure 18).

After finding the transits for the day that you want to examine you can write them in around the natal chart, but it may be easier just to look at them. It is not difficult to spot the aspects these passing planets are making to the planets and angles on your own chart. All details about the different kind of aspects and what they mean can be found later in this book.

Remember that all astrologers tend to call *everything* a planet, despite the fact that the Sun is a star, the Moon is a satellite and Chiron is a planetoid. Also keep in mind that the *angles* are the ascendant, descendant, midheaven and nadir.

If you are using a computer program, print out a list of the day's transits and maybe generate a chart that shows the natal chart inside the wheel and the transits on the outside.

NOVEMBER 1975

Day	Sid. T.	Sun	Moon	Merc.	Venus	Mars	Jup.	Saturn	Uranus	Nept.	Pluto	N.Node
1	2:38:39	7Sc56 20	2Li32	21Li40	21Vi31	2Cn27	17Ar17R	2Le48	3Sc 9	10Sg19	10Li13	22Sc30
2	2:42:35	8 56 23	17 28	23 10	22 28	2 31	17 10	2 49	3 12	10 21	10 16	22 26
3	2:46:32	9 56 28	2Sc24	24 42	23 26	2 34	17 3	2 51	3 16	10 23	10 18	22 23
4	2:50:29	10 56 35	17 11	26 15	24 25	2 37	16 56	2 52	3 20	10 25	10 20	22 20
5	2:54:25	11 56 43	1Sg42	27 49	25 24	2 39	16 50	2 53	3 24	10 27	10 22	22 17
6	2:58:21	12 56 54	15 50	29 24	26 23	2 39	16 43	2 54	3 27	10 29	10 24	22 14
7	3: 2:18	13 57 6	29 34	1Sc 0	27 23	2 40R	16 37	2 55	3 31	10 31	10 26	22 11
8	3: 6:15	14 57 20	12Cp53	2 36	28 24	2 39	16 31	2 56	3 35	10 33	10 28	22 7
9	3:10:11	15 57 35	25 47	4 13	29 25	2 37	16 24	2 57	3 39	10 35	10 30	22 4
10	3:14: 8	16 57 52	8Aq20	5 50	0Li26	2 34	16 19	2 57	3 42	10 37	10 32	22 1
11	3:18: 5	17 58 10	20 36	7 27	1 28	2 31	16 13	2 58	3 46	10 39	10 34	21 58
12	3:22: 1	18 58 30	2Pi39	9 4	2 30	2 27	16 7	2 58	3 50	10 41	10 36	21 55
13	3:25:57	19 58 51	14 33	10 41	3 32	2 22	16 2	2 58	3 53	10 43	10 38	21 51
14	3:29:54	20 59 13	26 24	12 18	4 35	2 15	15 56	2 58	3 57	10 46	10 40	21 48
15	3:33:50	21 59 37	8Ar15	13 55	5 38	2 9	15 51	2 58R	4 1	10 48	10 42	21 45
16	3:37:47	23 0 3	20 10	15 31	6 41	2 1	15 46	2 58	4 4	10 50	10 43	21 42
17	3:41:44	24 0 29	2Ta12	17 8	7 45	1 52	15 41	2 58	4 8	10 52	10 45	21 39
18	3:45:40	25 0 58	14 23	18 44	8 49	1 43	15 37	2 58	4 11	10 54	10 47	21 36
19	3:49:37	26 1 28	26 45	20 20	9 54	1 32	15 32	2 57	4 15	10 56	10 49	21 32
20	3:53:33	27 1 59	9Ge19	21 56	10 59	1 21	15 28	2 57	4 19	10 59	10 51	21 29
21	3:57:30	28 2 32	22 7	23 32	12 4	1 9	15 24	2 56	4 22	11 1	10 52	21 26
22	4: 1:26	29 3 7	5Cn 7	25 8	13 9	0 56	15 20	2 56	4 26	11 3	10 54	21 23
23	4: 5:23	0Sg 3 43	18 21	26 43	14 15	0 42	15 17	2 55	4 29	11 5	10 56	21 20
24	4: 9:20	1 4 21	1Le48	28 18	15 20	0 28	15 13	2 54	4 33	11 8	10 58	21 17
25	4:13:16	2 5 0	15 29	29 53	16 27	0 12	15 10	2 53	4 36	11 10	10 59	21 13
26	4:17:13	3 5 41	29 22	1Sg28	17 33	29Ge56	15 7	2 51	4 39	11 12	11 1	21 10
27	4:21: 9	4 6 24	13Vi28	3 3	18 40	29 39	15 4	2 50	4 43	11 14	11 2	21 7
28	4:25: 6	5 7 8	27 44	4 37	19 47	29 22	15 1	2 49	4 46	11 17	11 4	21 4
29	4:29: 2	6 7 54	12Li 8	6 12	20 54	29 4	14 59	2 47	4 50	11 19	11 5	21 1
30	4:32:59	7 8 42	26 36	7 46	22 1	28 45	14 56	2 45	4 53	11 21	11 7	20 57

11/22 Sun in Sag. 22:32 11/3 New 13:05(E) 11/10 1st Qt. 18:21 11/18 Full 22:29(E) 11/26 3rd Qt. 6:52

DECEMBER 1975

Day	Sid. T.	Sun	Moon	Merc.	Venus	Mars	Jup.	Saturn	Uranus	Nept.	Pluto	N.Node
1	4:36:55	8Sg 9 31	11Sc 6	9Sg20	23Li 9	28Ge25R	14Ar54R	2Le44R	4Sc56	11Sg23	11Li 9	20Sc54
2	4:40:52	9 10 21	25 30	10 54	24 16	28 5	14 52	2 42	5 0	11 26	11 10	20 51
3	4:44:49	10 11 13	9Sg44	12 29	25 24	27 45	14 51	2 40	5 3	11 28	11 11	20 48
4	4:48:45	11 12 6	23 43	14 3	26 33	27 23	14 49	2 38	5 6	11 30	11 13	20 45
5	4:52:42	12 13 0	7Cp22	15 37	27 41	27 2	14 48	2 36	5 9	11 32	11 14	20 42
6	4:56:38	13 13 55	20 41	17 11	28 50	26 40	14 47	2 33	5 13	11 35	11 16	20 38
7	5: 0:35	14 14 50	3Aq38	18 45	29 58	26 18	14 46	2 31	5 16	11 37	11 17	20 35
8	5: 4:31	15 15 47	16 14	20 19	1Sc 7	25 55	14 45	2 29	5 19	11 39	11 18	20 32
9	5: 8:28	16 16 44	28 33	21 53	2 17	25 32	14 45	2 26	5 22	11 41	11 19	20 29
10	5:12:25	17 17 41	10Pi37	23 27	3 26	25 9	14 45	2 23	5 25	11 44	11 21	20 26
11	5:16:21	18 18 40	22 33	25 1	4 35	24 46	14 45D	2 21	5 28	11 46	11 22	20 23
12	5:20:18	19 19 39	4Ar23	26 35	5 45	24 22	14 45	2 18	5 31	11 48	11 23	20 19
13	5:24:14	20 20 38	16 14	28 9	6 55	23 59	14 45	2 15	5 34	11 50	11 24	20 16
14	5:28:11	21 21 38	28 10	29 44	8 4	23 35	14 46	2 12	5 37	11 53	11 25	20 13
15	5:32: 7	22 22 39	10Ta16	1Cp18	9 14	23 12	14 47	2 9	5 40	11 55	11 26	20 10
16	5:36: 4	23 23 41	22 35	2 52	10 25	22 48	14 48	2 5	5 43	11 57	11 27	20 7
17	5:40: 0	24 24 43	5Ge10	4 27	11 35	22 25	14 49	2 2	5 45	11 59	11 28	20 3
18	5:43:57	25 25 45	18 2	6 1	12 45	22 2	14 51	1 59	5 48	12 2	11 29	20 0
19	5:47:54	26 26 48	1Cn12	7 35	13 56	21 39	14 52	1 55	5 51	12 4	11 30	19 57
20	5:51:50	27 27 52	14 39	9 9	15 7	21 17	14 54	1 52	5 54	12 6	11 31	19 54
21	5:55:46	28 28 56	28 20	10 44	16 17	20 55	14 56	1 48	5 56	12 8	11 32	19 51
22	5:59:43	29 30 1	12Le12	12 18	17 28	20 33	14 58	1 44	5 59	12 10	11 33	19 48
23	6: 3:40	0Cp31 7	26 13	13 52	18 39	20 11	15 1	1 41	6 1	12 13	11 34	19 44
24	6: 7:36	1 32 13	10Vi18	15 25	19 50	19 50	15 4	1 37	6 4	12 15	11 35	19 41
25	6:11:33	2 33 20	24 26	16 58	21 2	19 30	15 6	1 33	6 6	12 17	11 35	19 38
26	6:15:30	3 34 28	8Li34	18 31	22 13	19 10	15 9	1 29	6 9	12 19	11 36	19 35
27	6:19:26	4 35 36	22 41	20 3	23 24	18 50	15 13	1 25	6 11	12 21	11 37	19 32
28	6:23:23	5 36 45	6Sc45	21 34	24 36	18 31	15 16	1 20	6 14	12 23	11 37	19 28
29	6:27:19	6 37 55	20 46	23 5	25 48	18 13	15 20	1 16	6 16	12 25	11 38	19 25
30	6:31:16	7 39 5	4Sg42	24 34	26 59	17 56	15 24	1 12	6 18	12 27	11 38	19 22
31	6:35:12	8 40 15	18 29	26 1	28 11	17 39	15 28	1 8	6 21	12 30	11 39	19 19

12/22 Sun in Cap. 11:47 12/3 New 0:51 12/10 1st Qt. 14:40 12/18 Full 14:40 12/25 3rd Qt. 14:53

Figure 16 ***Sample pages from the*** **World Ephemeris for the 20th Century**

LONGITUDE SEPTEMBER 1982

DAY	SID.TIME	☉	☽	TRUE ☊	☿	♀	♂	♃	♄	♅	♆	♇
	h m s	° ' "	° ' "	° '	° '	° '	° '	° '	° '	° '	° '	° '
1	10 41 17	8♍ 43 15	15♒ 27 35	11♋R59.9	5♎ 17.1	22♌ 6.3	17♏ 40.7	6♏ 13.1	19♎ 43.4	0♐ 48.3	24♐R16.9	25♎ 3.5
2	10 45 14	9 41 19	27 49 26	11 52.8	6 24.5	23 20.2	18 19.4	6 22.8	19 49.5	0 49.5	24 16.7	25 5.3
3	10 49 11	10 39 24	10♓ 25 35	11 43.8	7 29.8	24 34.2	18 58.3	6 32.5	19 55.7	0 50.8	24 16.6	25 7.2
4	10 53 7	11 37 31	23 16 22	11 33.4	8 32.7	25 48.1	19 37.3	6 42.4	20 1.9	0 52.1	24 16.6	25 9.0
5	10 57 4	12 35 39	6♈ 21 13	11 22.7	9 33.2	27 2.1	20 16.5	6 52.3	20 8.1	0 53.5	24D 16.5	25 10.9
6	11 1 0	13 33 49	19 38 58	11 12.9	10 31.2	28 16.2	20 55.7	7 2.4	20 14.4	0 54.9	24 16.5	25 12.8
7	11 4 57	14 32 1	3♉ 8 13	11 4.9	11 26.4	29 30.3	21 35.1	7 12.5	20 20.8	0 56.3	24 16.6	25 14.8
8	11 8 53	15 30 16	16 47 39	10 59.3	12 18.7	0♍ 44.4	22 14.6	7 22.8	20 27.2	0 57.8	24 16.6	25 16.7
9	11 12 50	16 28 32	0♊ 36 16	10 56.3	13 7.9	1 58.5	22 54.3	7 33.1	20 33.6	0 59.4	24 16.7	25 18.7
10	11 16 46	17 26 50	14 33 24	10D 55.4	13 53.8	3 12.7	23 34.0	7 43.5	20 40.1	1 1.0	24 16.9	25 20.7
11	11 20 43	18 25 11	28 38 33	10 55.8	14 36.1	4 27.0	24 13.9	7 54.0	20 46.6	1 2.6	24 17.0	25 22.7
12	11 24 40	19 23 34	12♋ 50 56	10R 56.1	15 14.6	5 41.2	24 53.9	8 4.6	20 53.2	1 4.3	24 17.2	25 24.7
13	11 28 36	20 21 58	27 9 8	10 55.2	15 49.0	6 55.5	25 34.0	8 15.2	20 59.8	1 6.1	24 17.5	25 26.8
14	11 32 33	21 20 25	11♌ 30 34	10 52.0	16 19.0	8 9.9	26 14.3	8 26.0	21 6.4	1 7.9	24 17.7	25 28.8
15	11 36 29	22 18 54	25 51 23	10 46.0	16 44.3	9 24.2	26 54.6	8 36.8	21 13.1	1 9.7	24 18.0	25 30.9
16	11 40 26	23 17 25	10♍ 6 41	10 37.3	17 4.5	10 38.6	27 35.1	8 47.7	21 19.8	1 11.6	24 18.4	25 33.0
17	11 44 22	24 15 58	24 11 4	10 26.6	17 19.3	11 53.1	28 15.7	8 58.7	21 26.6	1 13.5	24 18.7	25 35.1
18	11 48 19	25 14 33	7♎ 59 28	10 14.8	17 28.4	13 7.5	28 56.4	9 9.8	21 33.3	1 15.5	24 19.1	25 37.3
19	11 52 15	26 13 9	21 28 4	10 3.1	17R 31.3	14 22.0	29 37.3	9 20.9	21 40.2	1 17.5	24 19.5	25 39.4
20	11 56 12	27 11 48	4♏ 34 49	9 52.8	17 27.7	15 36.5	0♐ 18.2	9 32.2	21 47.0	1 19.6	24 20.0	25 41.6
21	12 0 8	28 10 28	17 19 42	9 44.6	17 17.4	16 51.1	0 59.3	9 43.5	21 53.9	1 21.7	24 20.5	25 43.8
22	12 4 5	29 9 10	29 44 36	9 39.1	17 0.1	18 5.6	1 40.4	9 54.8	22 0.8	1 23.8	24 21.0	25 46.0
23	12 8 2	0♎ 7 54	11♐ 52 56	9 35.9	16 35.5	19 20.2	2 21.7	10 6.3	22 7.7	1 26.0	24 21.6	25 48.2
24	12 11 58	1 6 39	23 49 16	9 34.7	16 3.7	20 34.8	3 3.1	10 17.8	22 14.7	1 28.2	24 22.2	25 50.4
25	12 15 55	2 5 26	5♑ 38 48	9 34.5	15 24.7	21 49.5	3 44.5	10 29.3	22 21.7	1 30.5	24 22.8	25 52.7
26	12 19 51	3 4 15	17 27 4	9 34.3	14 38.8	23 4.1	4 26.1	10 41.0	22 28.7	1 32.8	24 23.5	25 54.9
27	12 23 48	4 3 6	29 19 31	9 33.0	13 46.5	24 18.8	5 7.8	10 52.7	22 35.7	1 35.2	24 24.2	25 57.2
28	12 27 44	5 1 59	11♒ 21 14	9 29.6	12 48.5	25 33.5	5 49.6	11 4.4	22 42.8	1 37.6	24 24.9	25 59.5
29	12 31 41	6 0 53	23 36 34	9 23.7	11 45.8	26 48.3	6 31.5	11 16.3	22 49.9	1 40.0	24 25.6	26 1.8
30	12 35 37	6♎ 59 49	6♓ 8 47	9♋ 15.1	10♎ 39.7	28♍ 3.0	7♐ 13.5	11♏ 28.1	22♎ 57.0	1♐ 42.5	24♐ 26.4	26♎ 4.1

LONGITUDE — OCTOBER 1982

DAY	SID.TIME	☉	☽	TRUE ☊	☿	♀	♂	♃	♄	♅	♆	♇
	h m s	° ' "	° ' "	° '	° '	° '	° '	° '	° '	° '	° '	° '
1	12 39 34	7♎ 58 46	18♓ 59 46	9♋R 4.1	9♎R31.5	29♍ 17.8	7♐ 55.5	11♏ 40.1	23♎ 4.1	1♐ 45.0	24♐ 27.2	26♎ 6.4
2	12 43 31	8 57 46	2♈ 9 49	8 51.5	8 23.1	0♎ 32.6	8 37.7	11 52.1	23 11.2	1 47.6	24 28.1	26 8.7
3	12 47 27	9 56 48	15 37 37	8 38.6	7 16.3	1 47.4	9 20.0	12 4.1	23 18.4	1 50.2	24 29.0	26 11.0
4	12 51 24	10 55 52	29 20 27	8 26.5	6 12.8	3 2.2	10 2.3	12 16.2	23 25.6	1 52.8	24 29.9	26 13.4
5	12 55 20	11 54 58	13♉ 14 41	8 16.4	5 14.4	4 17.1	10 44.8	12 28.4	23 32.8	1 55.5	24 30.8	26 15.7
6	12 59 17	12 54 6	27 16 29	8 9.1	4 22.8	5 32.0	11 27.3	12 40.6	23 40.0	1 58.2	24 31.8	26 18.1
7	13 3 13	13 53 17	11♊ 22 22	8 4.7	3 39.3	6 46.9	12 10.0	12 52.9	23 47.2	2 0.9	24 32.8	26 20.4
8	13 7 10	14 52 30	25 29 41	8 2.9	3 5.3	8 1.8	12 52.7	13 5.2	23 54.4	2 3.7	24 33.8	26 22.8
9	13 11 6	15 51 45	9♋ 36 43	8D 2.7	2 41.3	9 16.8	13 35.5	13 17.6	24 1.7	2 6.5	24 34.9	26 25.2
10	13 15 3	16 51 3	23 42 25	8R 2.7	2 28.0	10 31.7	14 18.4	13 30.0	24 8.9	2 9.3	24 36.0	26 27.6
11	13 19 0	17 50 23	7♌ 46 1	8 1.6	2D 25.6	11 46.7	15 1.5	13 42.4	24 16.2	2 12.2	24 37.1	26 29.9
12	13 22 56	18 49 45	21 46 35	7 58.3	2 34.0	13 1.8	15 44.6	13 54.9	24 23.5	2 15.1	24 38.3	26 32.3
13	13 26 53	19 49 9	5♍ 42 32	7 52.2	2 52.8	14 16.8	16 27.8	14 7.5	24 30.7	2 18.1	24 39.4	26 34.7
14	13 30 49	20 48 36	19 31 37	7 43.3	3 21.7	15 31.8	17 11.0	14 20.1	24 38.0	2 21.0	24 40.7	26 37.1
15	13 34 46	21 48 5	3♎ 11 0	7 32.1	4 0.0	16 46.9	17 54.4	14 32.7	24 45.3	2 24.0	24 41.9	26 39.5
16	13 38 42	22 47 36	16 37 37	7 19.8	4 46.9	18 2.0	18 37.9	14 45.4	24 52.6	2 27.1	24 43.2	26 41.9
17	13 42 39	23 47 9	29 48 51	7 7.5	5 41.7	19 17.1	19 21.4	14 58.1	24 59.9	2 30.1	24 44.5	26 44.4
18	13 46 35	24 46 44	12♏ 42 58	6 56.4	6 43.6	20 32.2	20 5.0	15 10.9	25 7.2	2 33.2	24 45.8	26 46.8
19	13 50 32	25 46 21	25 19 29	6 47.5	7 51.7	21 47.3	20 48.8	15 23.7	25 14.5	2 36.4	24 47.1	26 49.2
20	13 54 29	26 46 0	7♐ 39 22	6 41.3	9 5.3	23 2.4	21 32.6	15 36.5	25 21.8	2 39.5	24 48.5	26 51.6
21	13 58 25	27 45 41	19 45 0	6 37.7	10 23.7	24 17.6	22 16.4	15 49.3	25 29.1	2 42.7	24 49.9	26 54.0
22	14 2 22	28 45 24	1♑ 39 55	6D 36.2	11 46.1	25 32.7	23 0.4	16 2.2	25 36.4	2 45.9	24 51.4	26 56.4
23	14 6 18	29 45 8	13 28 37	6 36.2	13 12.0	26 47.9	23 44.4	16 15.1	25 43.7	2 49.1	24 52.8	26 58.8
24	14 10 15	0♏ 44 54	25 16 12	6R 36.7	14 40.8	28 3.1	24 28.5	16 28.1	25 51.0	2 52.4	24 54.3	27 1.3
25	14 14 11	1 44 42	7♒ 8 10	6 36.5	16 12.0	29 18.3	25 12.7	16 41.1	25 58.3	2 55.7	24 55.8	27 3.7
26	14 18 8	2 44 32	19 9 57	6 34.9	17 45.1	0♏ 33.5	25 57.0	16 54.1	26 5.6	2 59.0	24 57.4	27 6.1
27	14 22 4	3 44 23	1♓ 26 41	6 31.2	19 19.8	1 48.7	26 41.3	17 7.1	26 12.8	3 2.3	24 58.9	27 8.5
28	14 26 1	4 44 16	14 2 42	6 25.2	20 55.7	3 3.9	27 25.7	17 20.1	26 20.1	3 5.7	25 0.5	27 10.9
29	14 29 58	5 44 10	27 1 5	6 17.1	22 32.6	4 19.1	28 10.2	17 33.2	26 27.3	3 9.0	25 2.1	27 13.3
30	14 33 54	6 44 7	10♈ 23 7	6 7.6	24 10.3	5 34.3	28 54.8	17 46.3	26 34.6	3 12.4	25 3.8	27 15.7
31	14 37 51	7♏ 44 5	24♈ 8 3	5♋ 57.5	25♎ 48.5	6♏ 49.5	29♐ 39.4	17♏ 59.4	26♎ 41.8	3♐ 15.9	25♐ 5.4	27♎ 18.1

Figure 17 ***Sample pages from*** **The American Ephemeris for the 20th Century**

NEW MOON–June28. 0h.50m. am. (5°♋54′)

12					JUNE 1995				RAPHAEL'S	
D	D	Sidereal	⊙	⊙	☽	☽	☽	☽	Midnight	
M	W	Time	Long.	Dec.	Long.	Lat.	Dec.	Node	☽ Long.	☽ Dec.
		H. M. S.	° ′ ″	° ′	° ′ ″	° ′	° ′	° ′	° ′ ″	° ′
1	Th	4 38 0	10 ♊ 32 29	22 N 2	14 ♋ 21 51	4 S 51	17 N51	3 ♏ 45	20 ♋ 20 21	16 N56
2	F	4 41 57	11 30 0	22 10	26 20 30	5 7	15 51	3 41	2 ♌ 22 38	14 35
3	S	4 45 53	12 27 29	22 17	8 ♌ 27 8	5 10	13 9	3 38	14 34 22	11 34
4	Su	4 49 50	13 24 58	22 24	20 44 47	4 59	9 51	3 35	26 58 49	8 0
5	M	4 53 46	14 22 25	22 31	3 ♍ 16 55	4 33	6 3	3 32	9 ♍ 39 33	4 N 0
6	T	4 57 43	15 19 50	22 38	16 7 11	3 54	1 N53	3 29	22 40 16	0 S 17
7	W	5 1 40	16 17 15	22 44	29 19 11	3 1	2 S 30	3 25	6 ♎ 4 18	4 42
8	Th	5 5 36	17 14 38	22 50	12 ♎ 55 53	1 56	6 53	3 22	19 54 7	9 1
9	F	5 9 33	18 12 1	22 55	26 59 1	0 S 42	11 3	3 19	4 ♏ 10 29	12 58
10	S	5 13 29	19 9 22	23 0	11 ♏ 28 13	0 N36	14 42	3 16	18 51 45	16 13
11	Su	5 17 26	20 6 42	23 4	26 20 24	1 54	17 29	3 13	3 ♐ 53 16	18 28
12	M	5 21 22	21 4 2	23 8	11 ♐ 29 18	3 5	19 6	3 10	19 7 17	19 24
13	T	5 25 19	22 1 20	23 12	26 45 54	4 3	19 21	3 6	4 ♑ 23 48	18 56
14	W	5 29 15	22 58 38	23 15	11 ♑ 59 36	4 44	18 11	3 3	19 32 3	17 7
15	Th	5 33 12	23 55 56	23 18	26 59 58	5 5	15 46	3 0	4 ♒ 22 22	14 11
16	F	5 37 9	24 53 13	23 20	11 ♒ 38 28	5 5	12 24	2 57	18 47 43	10 28
17	S	5 41 5	25 50 29	23 22	25 49 45	4 46	8 25	2 54	2 ♓ 44 25	6 17
18	Su	5 45 2	26 47 46	23 24	9 ♓ 31 46	4 11	4 S 7	2 51	16 12 1	1 S 56
19	M	5 48 58	27 45 2	23 25	22 45 29	3 24	0 N15	2 47	29 12 36	2 N23
20	T	5 52 55	28 42 17	23 26	5 ♈ 33 53	2 28	4 28	2 44	11 ♈ 49 55	6 29
21	W	5 56 51	29 ♊ 39 33	23 26	18 1 16	1 26	8 23	2 41	24 8 33	10 12
22	Th	6 0 48	0 ♋ 36 48	23 26	0 ♉ 12 23	0 N21	11 53	2 38	6 ♉ 13 19	13 25
23	F	6 4 44	1 34 3	23 26	12 11 57	0 S 43	14 49	2 35	18 8 46	16 3
24	S	6 8 41	2 31 18	23 25	24 4 18	1 45	17 6	2 31	29 58 58	17 58
25	Su	6 12 38	3 28 33	23 24	5 ♊ 53 12	2 41	18 38	2 28	11 ♊ 47 20	19 7
26	M	6 16 34	4 25 48	23 22	17 41 42	3 31	19 22	2 25	23 36 35	19 25
27	T	6 20 31	5 23 2	23 20	29 32 14	4 11	19 15	2 22	5 ♋ 28 52	18 52
28	W	6 24 27	6 20 17	23 17	11 ♋ 26 41	4 41	18 17	2 19	17 25 51	17 29
29	Th	6 28 24	7 17 31	23 14	23 26 33	4 58	16 30	2 16	29 28 56	15 20
30	F	6 32 20	8 ♋ 14 44	23 N11	5 ♌ 33 11	5 S 3	13 N59	2 ♏ 12	11 ♌ 39 30	12 N29

D	Mercury			Venus			Mars			Jupiter	
M	Lat.	Dec.		Lat.	Dec.		Lat.	Dec.		Lat.	Dec.
	° ′	° ′	° ′	° ′	° ′	° ′	° ′	° ′	° ′	° ′	° ′
1	1 S 34	21 N 9	20 N 49	1 S 21	16 N 8	16 N29	1 N 19	11 N35	11 N 23	0 N 48	21 S 14
3	2 8	20 29	20 9	1 18	16 50	17 10	1 17	11 12	11 0	0 48	21 12
5	2 40	19 49	19 31	1 14	17 30	17 49	1 14	10 48	10 36	0 48	21 10
7	3 9	19 13	18 56	1 11	18 8	18 27	1 12	10 24	10 12	0 47	21 8
9	3 34	18 41	18 27	1 7	18 45	19 3	1 9	10 0	9 47	0 47	21 6
11	3 53	18 14	18 3	1 3	19 20	19 37	1 7	9 35	9 22	0 47	21 4
13	4 8	17 54	17 47	0 59	19 53	20 8	1 5	9 10	8 57	0 47	21 2
15	4 17	17 42	17 39	0 54	20 23	20 38	1 2	8 45	8 32	0 46	21 0
17	4 21	17 37	17 38	0 50	20 52	21 5	1 0	8 19	8 6	0 46	20 58
19	4 20	17 40	17 44	0 45	21 18	21 31	0 58	7 53	7 40	0 46	20 56
21	4 14	17 49	17 57	0 41	21 42	21 53	0 56	7 27	7 13	0 45	20 54
23	4 5	18 5	18 16	0 36	22 4	22 14	0 53	7 0	6 47	0 45	20 53
25	3 52	18 27	18 40	0 31	22 23	22 31	0 51	6 33	6 20	0 45	20 51
27	3 35	18 53	19 8	0 27	22 39	22 47	0 49	6 6	5 52	0 44	20 49
29	3 17	19 23	19 N 39	0 22	22 53	22 N59	0 47	5 39	5 N 25	0 44	20 48
31	2 S 56	19 N56		0 S 17	23 N 5		0 N 45	5 N11		0 N 43	20 S 46

FIRST QUARTER–June 6,10h.26m. am. (15°♍16′)

Figure 18 ***Sample pages from*** **Raphael's Astronomical Ephemeris**

FULL MOON-June13, 4h. 3m. am. (21°♐ 42′)

EPHEMERIS]				JUNE 1995														13
D	☿	♀	♂	♃	♄	♅	♆	♇	Lunar Aspects									
M	Long.	Long.	Long.	Long.	Long.	Long.	Long.	Long.	☉	☿	♀	♂	♃	♄	♅	♆	♇
	° ′	° ′	° ′	° ′	° ′	° ′	° ′	° ′									
1	16♊ 8	18♉50	3♍10	10♐ 31	23♓45	0♒11	25♑15	28♏54	⚺	⚺	⚹	∠					Q
2	15R 37	20 3	3 38	10R 23	23 49	0R 9	25R 14	28R 53	∠	∠			Q	△	☍	☍	△
3	15 5	21 16	4 7	10 15	23 52	0 8	25 12	28 51	⚹			⚺	△	Q			
4	14 32	22 29	4 36	10 8	23 55	0 7	25 11	28 49		⚹	□						
5	13 58	23 42	5 5	10 0	23 58	0 5	25 10	28 48				☌					□
6	13 25	24 55	5 35	9 53	24 1	0 4	25 9	28 46	□	□			□		Q	Q	
7	12 52	26 8	6 4	9 45	24 4	0 2	25 8	28 45			△			☍	△	△	⚹
8	12 21	27 21	6 34	9 38	24 7	0♒ 1	25 7	28 43	△	△	Q	⚺	⚹				∠
9	11 51	28 34	7 4	9 30	24 9	29♑59	25 6	28 42	Q	Q		∠	∠		□	□	⚺
10	11 24	29♉47	7 34	9 23	24 12	29 58	25 4	28 40				⚹	⚺	Q			
11	10 59	1♊ 0	8 4	9 15	24 14	29 56	25 3	28 39			☍			△	⚹	⚹	☌
12	10 38	2 13	8 34	9 8	24 17	29 54	25 2	28 37		☍		□	☌		∠	∠	
13	10 20	3 26	9 5	9 0	24 19	29 53	25 1	28 36	☍					□	⚺	⚺	⚺
14	10 6	4 39	9 35	8 53	24 21	29 51	24 59	28 34				△	⚺				∠
15	9 56	5 52	10 6	8 46	24 23	29 49	24 58	28 33		Q	Q	Q	∠	⚹	☌	☌	⚹
16	9 50	7 5	10 37	8 39	24 25	29 47	24 57	28 31	Q	△	△		⚹	∠			
17	9D 49	8 18	11 8	8 32	24 27	29 46	24 55	28 30	△					⚺	⚺	⚺	□
18	9 52	9 31	11 39	8 25	24 29	29 44	24 54	28 28		□	□	☍	□		∠	∠	
19	10 0	10 44	12 11	8 18	24 31	29 42	24 53	28 27	□					☌		⚹	△
20	10 12	11 57	12 42	8 11	24 33	29 40	24 51	28 26		⚹			△		⚹		
21	10 30	13 11	13 14	8 5	24 34	29 38	24 50	28 24			⚹		Q				Q
22	10 51	14 24	13 46	7 58	24 36	29 36	24 48	28 23	⚹	∠	∠	Q		⚺	□	□	
23	11 18	15 37	14 18	7 52	24 37	29 34	24 47	28 22	∠	⚺	⚺	△		∠			
24	11 49	16 50	14 50	7 45	24 38	29 32	24 45	28 20						⚹	△	△	☍
25	12 24	18 3	15 22	7 39	24 39	29 30	24 44	28 19	⚺				☍			Q	
26	13 4	19 17	15 55	7 33	24 40	29 28	24 42	28 18		☌	☌	□			Q		
27	13 49	20 30	16 27	7 27	24 41	29 26	24 41	28 16						□			
28	14 37	21 43	17 0	7 21	24 42	29 24	24 39	28 15	☌	⚺		⚹					Q
29	15 30	22 56	17 33	7 15	24 43	29 21	24 38	28 14			⚺		Q	△	☍	☍	△
30	16♊ 27	24♊ 10	18♍ 5	7♐ 9	24♓43	29♑19	24♑36	28♏13	⚺	∠	∠	∠	△	Q			

D	Saturn		Uranus		Neptune		Pluto	
M	Lat.	Dec.	Lat.	Dec.	Lat.	Dec.	Lat.	Dec.
	° ′	° ′	° ′	° ′	° ′	° ′	° ′	° ′
1	1S59	4S18	0S33	20S39	0N33	20S32	13N56	6S18
3	1 59	4 16	0 33	20 40	0 33	20 33	13 55	6 18
5	2 0	4 14	0 33	20 40	0 33	20 33	13 55	6 18
7	2 0	4 12	0 33	20 41	0 33	20 34	13 54	6 17
9	2 1	4 10	0 33	20 42	0 33	20 34	13 54	6 17
11	2 1	4 9	0 34	20 43	0 33	20 34	13 54	6 17
13	2 2	4 7	0 34	20 43	0 33	20 35	13 53	6 17
15	2 2	4 6	0 34	20 44	0 33	20 35	13 52	6 17
17	2 3	4 5	0 34	20 45	0 33	20 36	13 52	6 17
19	2 3	4 4	0 34	20 46	0 33	20 36	13 51	6 17
21	2 4	4 3	0 34	20 47	0 33	20 37	13 51	6 17
23	2 4	4 3	0 34	20 47	0 33	20 37	13 50	6 17
25	2 5	4 2	0 34	20 48	0 33	20 38	13 49	6 17
27	2 6	4 2	0 34	20 49	0 33	20 38	13 49	6 17
29	2 6	4 2	0 34	20 50	0 33	20 39	13 48	6 18
31	2S 7	4S 2	0S34	20S51	0N33	20S39	13N47	6S18

Mutual Aspects

1 ☉☍♃. ☉Q♆. ☿P♃.
2 ☿P♅.
3 ☿Q♅. ♃∠♆. ☿P♆.
5 ☉☌☿. ♀⚹♄.
6 ☉Q♅. ♀△♆.
7 ♂±♅.
9 ♀☍♇. ☿P♀.
10 ☉±♆. ♀△♅.
13 ♂□♃.
15 ☉□♄. ☉±♅. ☿□♂. ☿Q♆ ♀Q♄.
♂Q♆.
16 ☉▽♆. ♀P♅. ♀P♆.
17 ♀☍♃. ♀P♃. ☿Stat.
18 ☿☌♀. ☿Q♆. ♀Q♆.
20 ☉▽♇.
21 ☉▽♅. ♀□♂.
22 ♀Q♅.
23 ♂Q♅.
25 ☉Q♂.
26 ☉±♇. ♀±♆. ♂P♇.
27 ♂Q♇. ♄⚹♆. ♃P♅.
28 ☿Q♅.
29 ☉▽♃. ♀±♅.
30 ♀□♄. ♀▽♆.

LAST QUARTER-June19,10h. 1m. pm. (28°♓ 9′)

A cautionary note

Some astrologers believe that transits denote the things that happen to us and that are outside our control, while progressions reflect our inner changes of mood. Unfortunately, very little is cut and dried in astrology, so bear this in mind but don't consider it a golden rule.

Interpreting the transits

The interpretations are exactly the same for transits as they are for all forms of progression. This means that if you want to check the meaning of Venus opposite Jupiter by progression, or of Neptune passing over the descendant by transit, look up the relevant passages in chapters 26 and 27.

Planets move at different speeds, which means that a transit of the Moon can be over and done with in a few hours, while a Pluto transit will take a couple of years. On the other hand, when dealing with *progressions*, the slower-moving planets don't actually move very far during a person's lifetime, so the faster-moving planets are the ones you need to look at.

Your ephemeris may point to an interesting transit involving the Moon and any of those planets that are visible to the naked eye on a particular evening. If, when the time comes, the night happens to be a clear one, go outside and look, because I guarantee that you will feel a rush of excitement at seeing your ephemeris come to life in the sky.

An example of a sad event

The following chart belongs to my friend Jonathan Dee, who suffered a bereavement on 2 June 1993. Jon's partner had been ill with stomach trouble for some time but had not been aware of the potential gravity of the situation. A road accident in April meant a short spell in hospital, and it was the shock of this that brought the underlying problem to the surface. Over the next few weeks Jon's lover became progressively sicker and finally died on 2 June. Jonathan's chart at that time showed transiting Saturn slowing down before turning to retrograde motion at nought degrees of Pisces, opposing his natal Pluto at nought

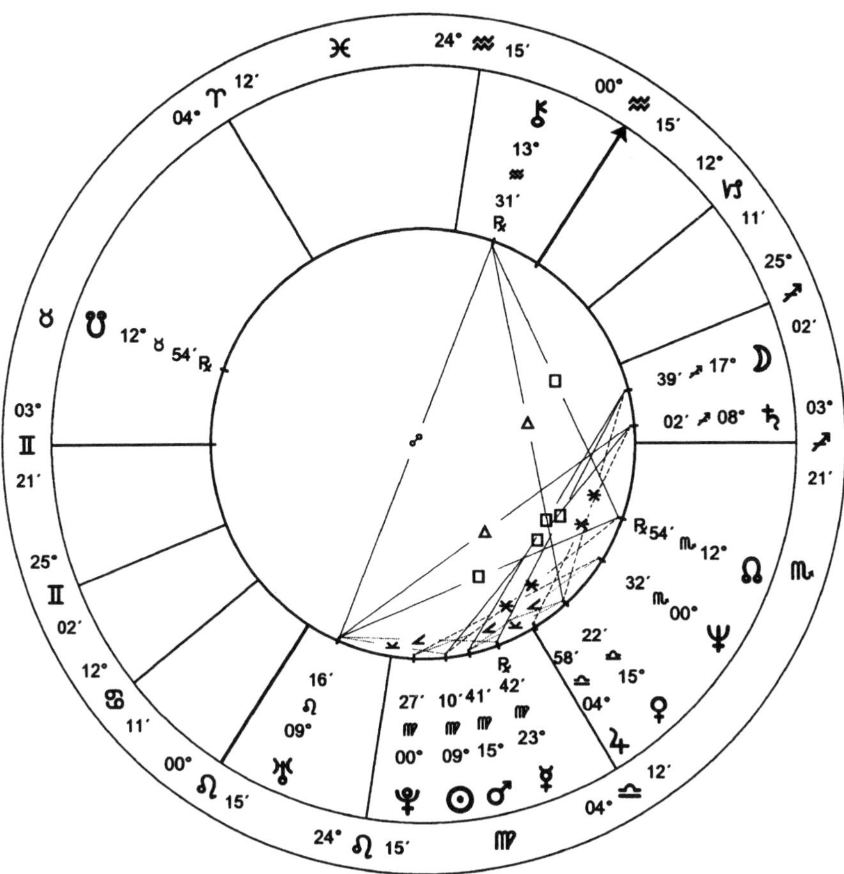

Figure 19 *A bad time in Jonathan's life*

Jonathan Dee
Natal Chart
Sep 1 1957
22.40 BST -1:00
Merthyr Tydfil, Wales
51N46 003W20

degrees of Virgo. Transiting Jupiter was conjunct natal Jupiter (the Jupiter return) and also moving from retrograde to direct motion. Transiting Mars was crossing Pluto, also at nought degrees of Virgo, and Venus was about to cross the south node.

JUNE 1993

Day	Sid. T.	Sun	Moon	Merc.	Venus	Mars	Jup.	Saturn	Uranus	Nept.	Pluto	N.Node
1	16:37:58	10Ge31 16	23Li47	27Ge57	25Ar 7	17Le28	4Li45R	0Pi16	21Cp41R	20Cp46R	23Sc41R	12Sg25
2	16:41:54	11 28 45	8Sc 8	29 43	26 0	18 1	4 45D	0 16	21 40	20 45	23 40	12 22
3	16:45:50	12 26 12	22 21	1Cn26	26 53	18 54	4 46	0 17	21 38	20 44	23 38	12 19
4	16:49:48	13 23 39	6Sg23	3 7	27 47	19 7	4 46	0 18	21 36	20 42	23 36	12 16
5	16:53:44	14 21 4	20 10	4 45	28 42	19 40	4 47	0 18	21 35	20 41	23 35	12 13
6	16:57:40	15 18 29	3Cp39	6 20	29 37	20 13	4 47	0 19	21 33	20 40	23 33	12 10
7	17: 1:37	16 15 53	16 49	7 52	0Ta33	20 46	4 48	0 19	21 31	20 39	23 32	12 6
8	17: 5:34	17 13 16	29 39	9 21	1 29	21 19	4 50	0 20	21 29	20 37	23 30	12 3
9	17: 9:30	18 10 38	12Aq11	10 48	2 25	21 53	4 51	0 20	21 27	20 36	23 29	12 0
10	17:13:27	19 8 0	24 28	12 11	3 22	22 26	4 52	0 20	21 25	20 35	23 27	11 57
11	17:17:23	20 5 21	6Pi33	13 32	4 20	23 0	4 54	0 20R	21 24	20 34	23 26	11 54
12	17:21:20	21 2 42	18 29	14 49	5 18	23 34	4 56	0 20	21 22	20 32	23 25	11 50
13	17:25:16	22 0 2	0Ar23	16 4	6 16	24 7	4 58	0 19	21 20	20 31	23 23	11 47
14	17:29:13	22 57 22	12 17	17 15	7 14	24 41	5 0	0 19	21 18	20 29	23 22	11 44
15	17:33: 9	23 54 41	24 17	18 23	8 13	25 15	5 3	0 19	21 16	20 28	23 20	11 41
16	17:37: 5	24 52 0	6Ta27	19 28	9 13	25 49	5 5	0 18	21 13	20 27	23 19	11 38
17	17:41: 3	25 49 19	18 50	20 30	10 12	26 23	5 8	0 18	21 11	20 25	23 18	11 35
18	17:44:59	26 46 37	1Ge29	21 28	11 12	26 57	5 11	0 17	21 9	20 24	23 16	11 31
19	17:48:56	27 43 55	14 26	22 23	12 13	27 31	5 14	0 16	21 7	20 22	23 15	11 28
20	17:52:52	28 41 12	27 42	23 15	13 13	28 6	5 17	0 15	21 5	20 21	23 14	11 25
21	17:56:49	29 38 29	11Cn16	24 2	14 14	28 40	5 20	0 14	21 3	20 19	23 12	11 22
22	18: 0:45	0Cn35 46	25 5	24 46	15 16	29 14	5 24	0 13	21 1	20 18	23 11	11 19
23	18: 4:41	1 33 2	9Le 7	25 26	16 17	29 49	5 28	0 12	20 58	20 16	23 10	11 16
24	18: 8:39	2 30 17	23 17	26 2	17 19	0Vi23	5 32	0 11	20 56	20 15	23 9	11 12
25	18:12:35	3 27 32	7Vi32	26 34	18 21	0 58	5 36	0 9	20 54	20 13	23 8	11 9
26	18:16:32	4 24 46	21 49	27 2	19 23	1 33	5 40	0 8	20 52	20 12	23 7	11 6
27	18:20:28	5 21 59	6Li 4	27 26	20 26	2 8	5 44	0 6	20 49	20 10	23 5	11 3
28	18:24:24	6 19 12	20 14	27 45	21 29	2 42	5 49	0 4	20 47	20 9	23 4	11 0
29	18:28:21	7 16 24	4Sc18	27 59	22 32	3 17	5 53	0 3	20 45	20 7	23 3	10 56
30	18:32:17	8 13 36	18 14	28 9	23 35	3 52	5 58	0 1	20 42	20 6	23 2	10 53

6/21 Sun In Can. 9:01 6/4 Full 13:03(E) 6/12 3rd Qt. 5:37 6/20 New 1:54 6/26 1st Qt. 22:45

Figure 20 **Transits for June 1993 when Jonathan Dee's partner died**

Bear in mind that a retrograde transit is never easy to live with and that Saturn, Pluto and Mars can all be considered to be 'malefic' planets. All three of these were either natally or transiting on an axis of nought degrees of Pisces and Virgo. Jupiter can be a happy-go-lucky planet but it can also be a difficult one, especially if other features on the chart are causing difficulties. Venus can indicate partnership matters and the nodes can indicate a *karmic* or unavoidably fated event.

8

Solar and Lunar Returns

Solar returns

SOLAR RETURNS are also sometimes known as solar return directions, and they are a form of transit, so they can be read in much the same way as any other list of transits. I think these are easiest to interpret when they are read as a stand-alone chart, rather than being put against a natal chart. Please try both methods for yourself before you make up your mind.

A solar return is arrived at by taking the Sun back to the exact spot that it occupied at the time of a subject's birth. This usually happens on the subject's birthday but it can occur a day before or afterwards. In plain English, it shows where the planets actually are in the sky at the time of the Sun's return, and this is, of course, a picture of the *transits* at the moment that the Sun returns to its natal position.

Solar returns are extremely awkward to do by hand, because you need to work out the exact moment of the return and then alter everything else on the chart to fit. However, this is very easy to do on a computer, and all good astrological programs include solar returns. Whatever program you have, simply request 'solar returns' from your menu and then follow the instructions. Most programs will ask you if you want the solar return for the place of birth or if you want to relocate. This simply means that if your client was born in one place and is now living somewhere else that you enter the coordinates for the new place.

Precession

Some programs ask you if you want to take 'precession' into account. Precession is a slight backwards movement of Earth that occurs over a period of time. Some astrologers use this precession feature, others don't. I suggest that you try both and see what works best for you.

What to look for

The solar return offers a flavour of the year from one birthday to the next. Start your interpretation by looking at it in its own right, rather than against the natal chart. The most important thing to look at is the new ascendant and the new midheaven, because these alone will tell you what kind of a year you are looking at. If, for example, the new ascendant at the time of the solar return is in Capricorn, this denotes an excellent year for work and ambition. However, it may be a stressful year, in which nothing comes easily but much will be learned. A radical change of midheaven could signify a major change of direction, even if only for the year in question. Otherwise, see what houses the solar return planets fall into and generally assess the chart for that year.

Now follow this up by working out any aspects that are formed between the solar return and the natal planets and angles. The chances are that your computer program will throw up a nice list of aspects if you ask it to.

An example of a solar return chart

Figure 21 shows the natal chart for my friend Anne Christie and the solar return chart (with precession) for her birthday on 19 July 1994.

During the year 1994–5 Anne was running her own business, which comprised two Montessori nursery schools. She began the year fit and well except for a nagging pain and slight swelling in her left foot. During the next few weeks this became much worse and, as a result, Anne paid a number of visits to her doctor and the local hospital. It became apparent that none of the doctors really knew what was wrong with

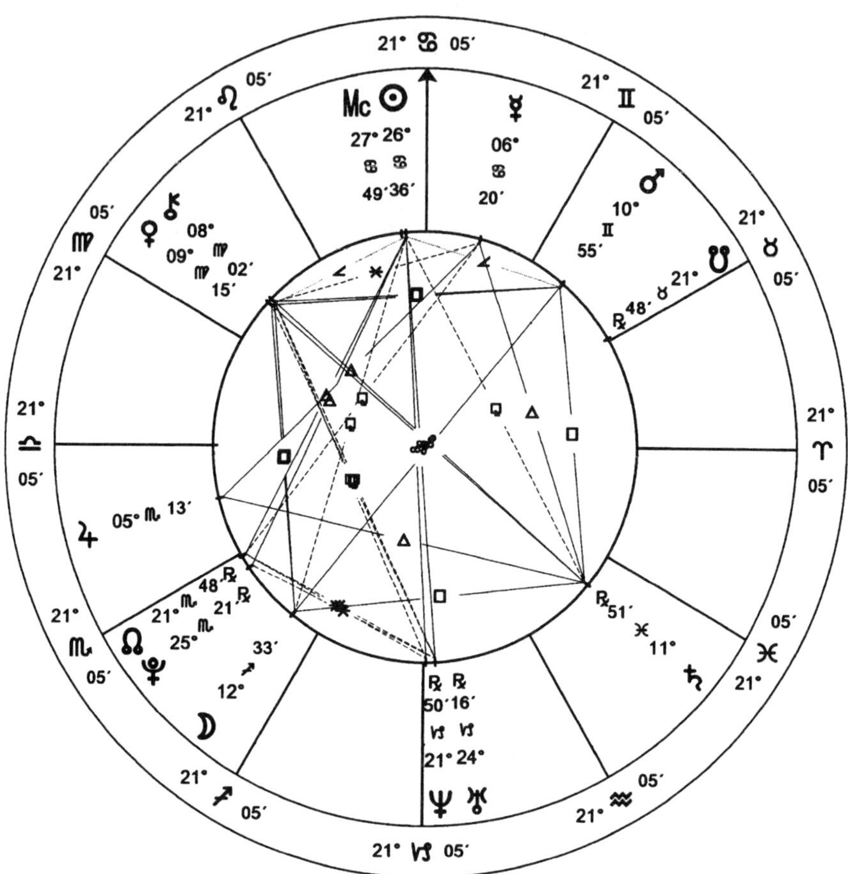

Figure 21 ***Anne Christie, solar return precessed***

Anne Christie
Solar Return Precessed
Jul 19 1994 (+- 20*secs*)
13:12:04 BST -1:00
Carshalton, England
51N22 000W10

her foot, until she eventually found her way to a top orthopaedic specialist. In December she had an operation to free a trapped tendon in her ankle and, at the time of writing, she is on the way to recovery.

Anne's solar return chart has a Libran ascendant, indicating that she would neither be living nor working alone in 1994–5. In fact, Anne is married, with her family all near at hand, and she works among many people. The Cancerian midheaven with the Sun close by indicates working in a caring profession (Cancer), probably teaching children (Cancer and Leo). Her descendant (relationships) is in Aries and her husband is an Arian. Her sixth house of health is empty but it has Pisces on its cusp (Pisces rules the feet). Uranus in Capricorn is opposing her Sun, suggesting unexpected problems (Uranus rules unexpected events and, incidentally, the ankles). The pain in her foot also affected her knee (Capricorn rules the knees). Neptune is opposite her Sun as well, and this suggests that her problems are mysterious and hard to diagnose (Neptune rules the feet). The main problem, of course, was the pain and swelling caused by the water that was collecting around the wounded tendon (Neptune rules fluids). Chiron and Saturn are in opposition and, although you are probably aware that Saturn rules the knees, the bones and chronic conditions, you may not be aware that the Roman god Chiron had a wounded knee and couldn't walk! The Moon opposite Mars suggests surgery, and as the Moon is in Sagittarius one could speculate that Anne would have to wait until the Sun was also in Sagittarius before having her foot operated on. In fact, she first saw the specialist as the Sun in Sagittarius opposed her Mars, and the decision to operate was made just as the Sun in Sagittarius crossed the solar return Moon at 12 degrees of Sagittarius! I have often noticed that the Moon is a trigger when dealing with acute health matters.

I haven't bothered to assess this solar return chart against the natal chart because, quite frankly, the whole story of Anne and her foot is there in the solar return chart for all to see.

Lunar returns

Lunar returns are exactly the same as solar returns but they occur every lunar month (27.32 days). The idea is that the Moon returns to the exact position that it occupied at the subject's birth, and the remaining chart is worked out around this. As this occurs every month, this will give a close-up view of the month in question in the same way that the solar return does for the year in question.

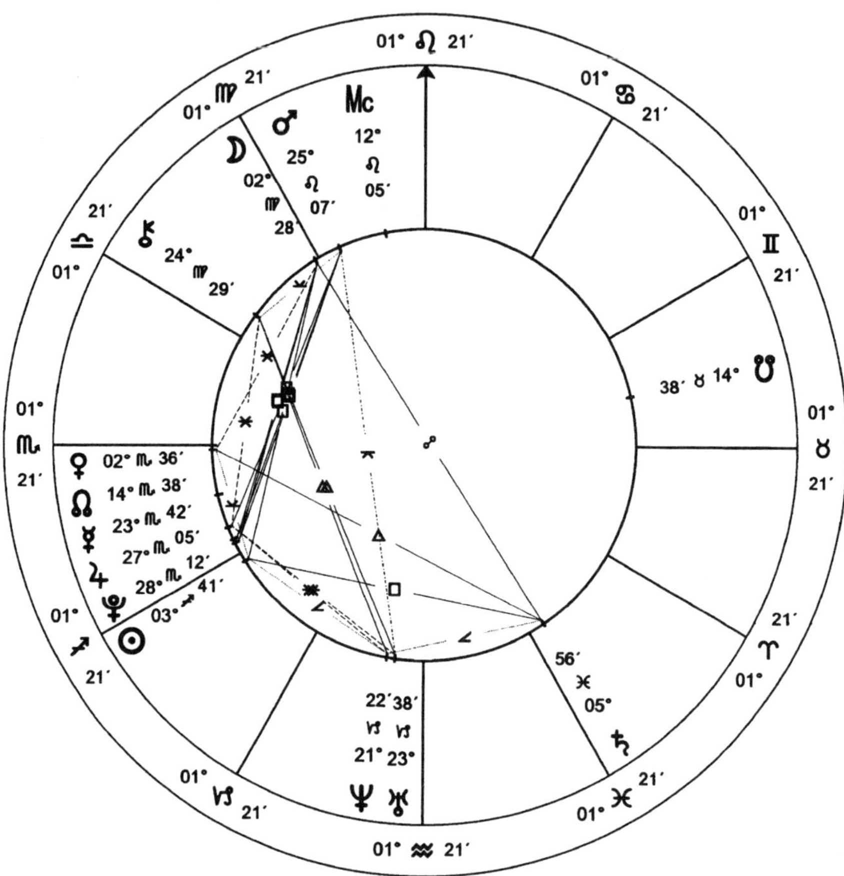

Figure 22 Anne Christie, lunar return precessed

Anne's lunar return chart

The chart shown in figure 22 is Anne's lunar return from 26 November to 24 December 1994, and it covers the period of her operation and her return home on crutches. The most obvious thing about this chart is the stellium (group of planets) in Scorpio. Scorpio rules surgeons and surgery. The Sun, Pluto, Jupiter and Mercury are all square to Mars and the

Moon, indicating something pretty drastic occurring. Remember that both Pluto and Mars indicate surgery. Chiron is trine to Uranus and Neptune, suggesting that the surgery would be successful. Aries, which is ruled by Mars and therefore connected to the idea of surgery, is on the cusp of the sixth house of health. Venus rules, among other things, the motor nerves, and thus the ability to move around. Anne's Venus is well aspected, with a sextile to Mars (surgeons) and a trine to Saturn (also surgeons, if you accept Michel Gauquelin's theories). The outlook seems to be good.

My friend Jonathan Dee has been experimenting with lunar returns, and he maintains that the effects are evident from about a week before it becomes exact until about three weeks afterwards. Jonathan has also discovered that these are an extremely effective way of focusing on an event that is very short term or fleeting. This is really quite a handy astrological tool, because so much astrology is too wide in its scope and its timescale to focus itself in this way.

9

The Solar Arc Method

THIS IS the first true method of planetary progression in this book, because, up to now, we have been looking at various forms of transit. The difference is that these progressions are not shown by the planets and stars in the sky, but by a mathematical manipulation of the subject's chart. Fortunately, the maths in this method is practically non-existent and it is extremely easy to do by hand. Incidentally, some astrologers call these solar arc directions rather than progressions; it doesn't matter, either name will do.

True solar arc progressions mean that every planet in addition to the ascendant and the midheaven moves forward at the same speed during one year as the Sun does during one day – that is, 57 minutes of a degree per day. If you are doing this by hand, simply progress everything on the chart forward by one whole degree per year and don't worry about the slight discrepancy at this stage.

The method – using HRH Prince Edward's chart

Starting with the natal chart, move each planet, the ascendant and the midheaven forward by one degree for each year of life to the point that you want to examine. If you want to look at what happened to someone at the age of 33, progress everything by 33 degrees. Some astrologers will tell you that this is not the best way to progress the ascendant and, to be honest, they are right. However, it will do for now. Once you have done this, place the new planets around the natal chart, mark in the new ascendant and midheaven, but leave the houses as per the natal chart. Now check to see if anything has moved into a new sign or house or if anything is making an aspect to anything else.

If you are using a computer program, then ask for 'solar arc progressions/directions' and follow the instructions. If you can put your progressions outside the natal chart do so; if not, produce the natal chart and a list of the progressions and put them around the chart by hand.

Converse progressions

Solar arc progressions can be worked backwards as well as forwards! This may sound crazy but there are astrologers who experiment with this method, even if they don't use it on their clients. If you want to look at the converse picture, then simply regress each planet by one degree. Or, in plain English, push each planet backwards by one degree per year.

What to look for

Whether direct or converse, check for changes of sign or house or any aspects that are being made between planets, angles or anything else that looks interesting.

A sample chart

The sample chart in figure 23 is for Prince Edward, who was born on 19 March 1964, and the chart is progressed to 19 March 1995, when he was 31. You may notice that the computer printout is headed 'Solar Arc Directed Chart', but this is just another name for the same thing. The outermost ring of the chart shows the natal position of the ascendant, the midheaven and the houses. The middle ring shows the solar arc progressions and the inner ring shows the natal chart itself. The program also produces the very helpful list of aspects between 'chart B', which is the progressed chart, and 'chart A', the natal one.

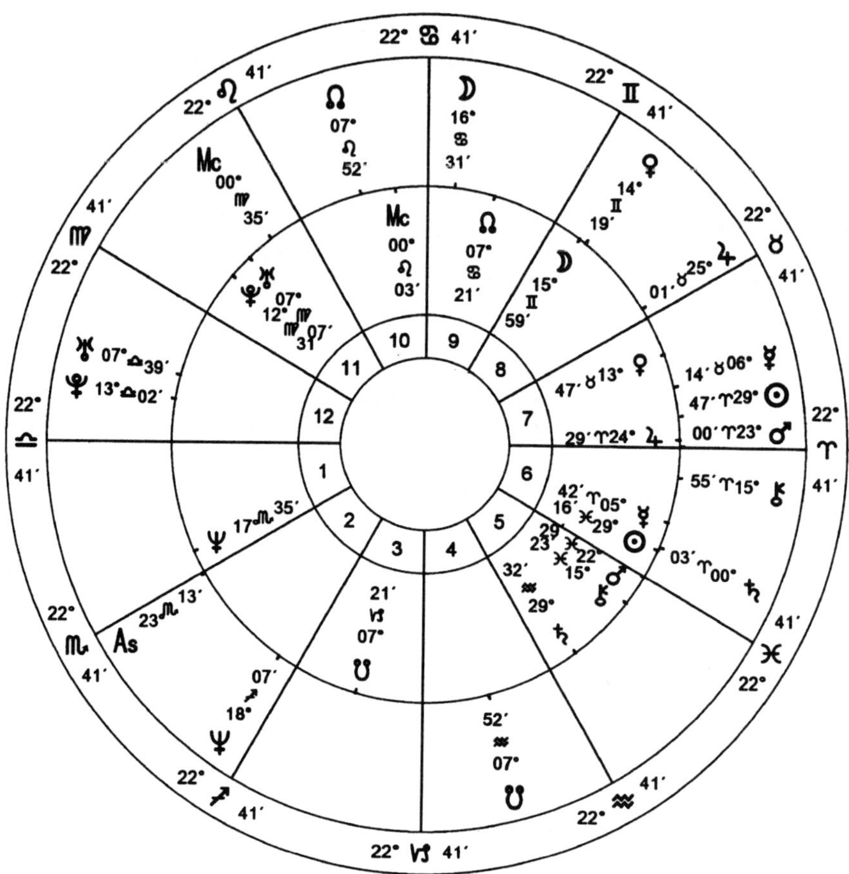

Figure 23 HRH Prince Edward, solar arc directed chart (outer wheel)

HRH Prince Edward
Solar Arc Directed Chart
Mar 19 1995
20:20 GMT +0:00
London, England

In 31 years, the planets will move almost 31 degrees from their natal positions. If you look carefully at the minutes of the degrees, you will notice that the planets have moved slightly less than this. This is because the computer takes account of the Sun's actual daily movement of 57 minutes of a degree, rather than taking a round figure of one whole degree.

You will notice that all the planets have changed signs and houses, which makes it easy to spot those areas of Prince Edward's life that are increasing or decreasing in importance. If I were sitting down with Prince Edward and talking to him about his chart I would give a detailed explanation about everything, but for the purposes of this interpretation I shall pick out only the important features. However, you will soon notice a phenomenon that is peculiar to astrology, and that is that almost all the planetary movements seem to be saying the same thing. I remember an excellent astrologer called Chryss Craswell once telling me, that in comparison to the tarot, astrology is like taking a steam-roller to crack a nut!

Interpreting Prince Edward's Chart

The Sun

Progressed to seventh house:	Relationships and partnerships of all kinds are important now. A calmer and more pleasant outlook and a nicer life style. Less emphasis on what others think of him. A chance to take his life into his own hands and to share it with others who have similar outlooks to himself.
Semi-sextile itself:	Changes within the past year; these should be fairly fortunate.
Sextile Saturn:	A time of hard work and extra responsibility, but this is happily shouldered and successful in its outcome.
Semi-square Chiron:	Could be some health problems. Chiron in Pisces in the fifth house suggests heart or back problems or maybe trouble with his feet. (Chiron natally conjunct Mars denotes sudden painful events.) This could also indicate something odd to do with children or young people.

The Moon	
Progressed to ninth house:	Travel, education, foreigners, legal and spiritual matters become important. Could have changed his outlook early in life when the Moon moved to the ninth.
Semi-sextile itself:	As with all the planets, a time of change, probably fortunate.
Parallel itself:	Big emotional event occurring now. Could be marriage and setting up of own home or business.
Parallel Pluto:	Major emotional event. Involves money, partnerships, sex, etc.

Mercury	
Progressed to seventh house:	Business and other relationships. Communicating with others. Also check back to what I said about the Sun progressed to the seventh.
Semi-sextile itself:	Ditto the previous semi-sextiles.
Contra-parallel Saturn:	Could be a break with the past, could be a desire to have children. Responsibilities happily shouldered. Slight but chronic health worry; could be backache or something to do with youngsters.
Trine Uranus:	Terrific changes for the better. Unusual events and sudden changes in direction. Friends, business associates and others are very helpful. A joyful time with unforeseeable happy events.

Venus	
Progressed to eighth house:	Money, business, sex, relationship.

Semi-sextile itself:	As per other planets.
Mars	
Progressed to seventh house:	Guess what? Partnerships, marriage, etc. Check back to what was said about the Sun progressed to the seventh.
Semi-sextile itself:	Time of action, change for the better but also of challenges.
Parallel Jupiter:	Luck with partnerships, money, sex, etc. (natal Jupiter in seventh).
Sesqui-quadrate Uranus:	Someone or something could let him down this year. It could be a back problem (Uranus in the eleventh, opposite a space between Chiron and Saturn in the fifth). Also children and youngsters.

At this point, I shall leave this interpretation because it is well on the way to becoming boring. Prince Edward has reached adulthood and is becoming an even more pleasant and cooperative person than he was at birth. He wants to get on well with people both at home and at work and he seems to be progressing towards a satisfactory relationship situation. There may be a slight health problem, possibly backache of some kind, and he may have a little trouble persuading his present girlfriend to have children. If the lady who is currently in his life does not want to marry and have a family, the energies that the planets appear to be exerting on him would lead him to find someone else who did! However, without actually talking to him or to his 'intended', this can only be speculation on my part.

10

Day-for-a-Year Progressions

I HAVE CHOSEN to call these progressions by their common, old-fashioned British name because the word 'progressions' tells us exactly what they are. When chatting to other astrologers, I may use the terms secondary progressions, secondary directions, directions or progressions. Other astrologers may even have a few more names for them!

Doing these by hand

If you are happy to work out a natal chart by hand, you won't find this technique difficult. The method that I outline here is rough and ready because it will take you only to the nearest *whole degree* of each planet. If you really do need to know the exact *degree and minute* of each planet, you should use a computer.

The example that I am using is for an imaginary person born in London, England, at 10 pm on 1 July 1960.

1. The first step is to make up a natal chart in the usual way.
2. Now turn to the line on the ephemeris that corresponds to the day of birth and mark this with a small coloured dot. The example below shows a birthdate of 1 July 1960. Now move your finger down to the next day and call this 1961. (The one after that will be 1962, etc.) When you reach the year that you want to examine, mark this with another small dot (see figure 24).

3. Now note down the new planetary positions. The progression in the example comes to 7 August 1960. (This becomes the equivalent of 1 July 1997.)
4. You will now have to make the same kinds of adjustments to the planets that you did on the natal chart. Thus, if your subject was born late in the day and any of the personal planets (the Sun, Mercury, Venus or Mars) are nearing the end of a particular degree on the day in question, simply push them over into the next one. Remember that, if you use a midnight ephemeris, the planets can move quite a bit by the time you reach your subject's birth time. For our example, we will assume that our subject was born at 10 pm.
5. Be careful to bear in mind that there may be planets that have turned to retrograde motion by the time you get down to the progressed date. If so, give them a backwards shove if necessary! In our example there are two retrograde planets, and Venus is so close to the end of a degree that it definitely warrants pushing over into the next one (see figure 25).
6. The Moon will definitely have to be adjusted because it moves half a degree for every hour of time. Thus, if your subject was born at 6 am, the Moon would be three degrees forward on the position shown in the ephemeris. If they were born at 6 pm, the Moon would be nine degrees forward of your ephemeris position. In our example the subject was born at 10 pm, which is 22 hours after midnight, therefore 11 degrees will have to be added to the natal Moon position (see figure 26).
7. If you are content to look at your subject's progressions for the time around their birthday, then leave things as they are, but, if you want to work a few months backwards or forwards from the birthday, then simply move the Moon forwards or backwards one degree per month.
8. There are various ways of recalculating the midheaven and the ascendant, but this is the easiest and the most effective. Note down the midheaven as shown on the natal chart and find it on your table of houses (remembering to trace the correct latitude for the place of birth) in the same way that you did when erecting the original natal chart.

JULY 1960

Day	Sid. T.	Sun	Moon	Merc.	Venus	Mars	Jup.	Saturn	Uranus	Nept.	Pluto	N.Node
·1	18:36:11	9Cn 9 11	25Vi21	29Cn59	11Cn26	7Ta42	27Sg22R	15Cp35R	18Le49	6Sc27R	4Vi 7	19Vi 5
2	18:40: 7	10 6 23	8Li11	0Le 9	12 40	8 25	27 14	15 31	18 53	6 26	4 8	19 2
3	18:44: 4	11 3 35	21 25	0 14	13 54	9 8	27 7	15 26	18 56	6 26	4 10	18 59
4	18:48: 1	12 0 46	5Sc 6	0 14R	15 8	9 50	27 0	15 22	18 59	6 25	4 11	18 56
5	18:51:57	12 57 57	19 16	0 10	16 21	10 33	26 52	15 18	19 2	6 25	4 13	18 53
6	18:55:54	13 55 8	3Sg52	0 1	17 35	11 16	26 45	15 13	19 5	6 24	4 14	18 49
7	18:59:51	14 52 19	18 52	29Cn47	18 49	11 59	26 39	15 9	19 8	6 24	4 15	18 46
8	19: 3:47	15 49 30	4Cp 6	29 29	20 3	12 41	26 32	15 4	19 12	6 24	4 17	18 43
9	19: 7:43	16 46 41	19 24	29 7	21 17	13 23	26 25	15 0	19 15	6 23	4 18	18 40
10	19:11:40	17 43 52	4Aq35	28 41	22 30	14 6	26 18	14 55	19 18	6 23	4 20	18 37
11	19:15:37	18 41 3	19 29	28 11	23 44	14 48	26 12	14 51	19 21	6 23	4 21	18 33
12	19:19:33	19 38 15	4Pi 0	27 39	24 58	15 30	26 5	14 47	19 25	6 23	4 23	18 30
13	19:23:30	20 35 27	18 2	27 3	26 12	16 12	25 59	14 42	19 28	6 22	4 24	18 27
14	19:27:27	21 32 39	1Ar36	26 26	27 26	16 54	25 53	14 38	19 32	6 22	4 26	18 24
15	19:31:23	22 29 53	14 44	25 47	28 39	17 36	25 46	14 34	19 35	6 22	4 28	18 21
16	19:35:20	23 27 6	27 29	25 7	29 53	18 18	25 40	14 29	19 38	6 22	4 29	18 18
17	19:39:16	24 24 21	9Ta56	24 27	1Le 7	19 0	25 34	14 25	19 42	6 22	4 31	18 14
18	19:43:12	25 21 36	22 8	23 47	2 21	19 41	25 29	14 21	19 45	6 22	4 32	18 11
19	19:47: 9	26 18 52	4Ge10	23 9	3 35	20 23	25 23	14 16	19 49	6 22D	4 34	18 8
20	19:51: 6	27 16 8	16 5	22 32	4 49	21 4	25 17	14 12	19 52	6 22	4 36	18 5
21	19:55: 2	28 13 26	27 57	21 58	6 2	21 45	25 12	14 8	19 56	6 22	4 37	18 2
22	19:58:59	29 10 43	9Cn48	21 27	7 16	22 27	25 7	14 4	19 59	6 22	4 39	17 59
23	20: 2:56	0Le 8 2	21 41	21 0	8 30	23 8	25 2	13 59	20 3	6 22	4 41	17 55
24	20: 6:52	1 5 21	3Le36	20 37	9 44	23 49	24 57	13 55	20 7	6 22	4 43	17 52
25	20:10:48	2 2 41	15 36	20 19	10 58	24 30	24 52	13 51	20 10	6 23	4 44	17 49
26	20:14:45	3 0 1	27 42	20 7	12 12	25 10	24 47	13 47	20 14	6 23	4 46	17 46
27	20:18:42	3 57 22	9Vi57	19 59	13 26	25 51	24 43	13 43	20 17	6 23	4 48	17 43
28	20:22:38	4 54 43	22 22	19 58D	14 40	26 32	24 39	13 39	20 21	6 23	4 50	17 39
29	20:26:35	5 52 5	5Li 0	20 2	15 54	27 12	24 34	13 35	20 25	6 24	4 52	17 36
30	20:30:32	6 49 28	17 55	20 13	17 7	27 52	24 30	13 31	20 28	6 24	4 53	17 33
31	20:34:28	7 46 51	1Sc10	20 30	18 21	28 33	24 27	13 27	20 32	6 24	4 55	17 30

7/22 Sun In Leo 20:38 7/2 1st Qt. 3:49 7/8 Full 19:37 7/15 3rd Qt. 15:43 7/23 New 18:31 7/31 1st Qt. 12:39

AUGUST 1960

Day	Sid. T.	Sun	Moon	Merc.	Venus	Mars	Jup.	Saturn	Uranus	Nept.	Pluto	N.Node
1	20:38:24	8Le44 15	14Sc46	20Cn53	19Le35	29Ta13	24Sg23R	13Cp24R	20Le36	6Sc25	4Vi57	17Vi27
2	20:42:21	9 41 39	28 46	21 22	20 49	29 53	24 19	13 20	20 39	6 25	4 59	17 24
3	20:46:17	10 39 4	13Sg 9	21 58	22 3	0Ge33	24 16	13 16	20 43	6 26	5 1	17 20
4	20:50:14	11 36 29	27 52	22 40	23 17	1 12	24 13	13 13	20 47	6 26	5 3	17 17
5	20:54:10	12 33 56	12Cp50	23 28	24 31	1 52	24 10	13 9	20 50	6 27	5 5	17 14
6	20:58: 7	13 31 23	27 54	24 23	25 45	2 31	24 7	13 6	20 54	6 28	5 6	17 11
· 7	21: 2: 4	14 28 51	12Aq55	25 23	26 59	3 11	24 5	13 2	20 58	6 28	5 8	17 8
8	21: 6: 0	15 26 20	27 44	26 29	28 12	3 50	24 2	12 59	21 1	6 29	5 10	17 5
9	21: 9:57	16 23 50	12Pi14	27 41	29 26	4 29	24 0	12 55	21 5	6 29	5 12	17 1
10	21:13:53	17 21 21	26 20	28 59	0Vi40	5 8	23 58	12 52	21 9	6 30	5 14	16 58
11	21:17:50	18 18 54	10Ar 0	0Le22	1 54	5 47	23 56	12 49	21 13	6 31	5 16	16 55
12	21:21:47	19 16 27	23 13	1 50	3 8	6 25	23 54	12 46	21 16	6 32	5 18	16 52
13	21:25:43	20 14 3	6Ta 3	3 22	4 22	7 4	23 53	12 43	21 20	6 32	5 20	16 49
14	21:29:40	21 11 40	18 32	4 59	5 36	7 42	23 51	12 40	21 24	6 33	5 22	16 45
15	21:33:36	22 9 18	0Ge46	6 40	6 50	8 21	23 50	12 37	21 28	6 34	5 24	16 42
16	21:37:33	23 6 58	12 48	8 25	8 4	8 59	23 49	12 34	21 31	6 35	5 26	16 39
17	21:41:29	24 4 40	24 42	10 13	9 18	9 37	23 48	12 31	21 35	6 36	5 28	16 36
18	21:45:26	25 2 23	6Cn34	12 3	10 32	10 15	23 48	12 29	21 39	6 37	5 30	16 33
19	21:49:22	26 0 8	18 26	13 57	11 45	10 52	23 47	12 26	21 43	6 38	5 32	16 30
20	21:53:19	26 57 54	0Le21	15 52	12 59	11 30	23 47	12 24	21 46	6 39	5 34	16 26
21	21:57:15	27 55 42	12 23	17 49	14 13	12 7	23 47D	12 21	21 50	6 40	5 36	16 23
22	22: 1:12	28 53 31	24 32	19 47	15 27	12 45	23 47	12 19	21 54	6 41	5 38	16 20
23	22: 5: 9	29 51 21	6Vi51	21 46	16 41	13 22	23 48	12 17	21 57	6 42	5 40	16 17
24	22: 9: 5	0Vi49 13	19 21	23 45	17 55	13 59	23 48	12 14	22 1	6 43	5 42	16 14
25	22:13: 2	1 47 6	2Li 3	25 45	19 9	14 35	23 49	12 12	22 5	6 44	5 44	16 11
26	22:16:58	2 45 1	14 58	27 45	20 23	15 12	23 50	12 10	22 8	6 46	5 46	16 7
27	22:20:55	3 42 57	28 7	29 44	21 37	15 48	23 51	12 8	22 12	6 47	5 48	16 4
28	22:24:51	4 40 54	11Sc32	1Vi43	22 51	16 25	23 52	12 6	22 16	6 48	5 50	16 1
29	22:28:48	5 38 53	25 12	3 41	24 5	17 1	23 53	12 5	22 20	6 49	5 52	15 58
30	22:32:45	6 36 53	9Sg 8	5 39	25 18	17 36	23 55	12 3	22 23	6 51	5 54	15 55
31	22:36:41	7 34 55	23 20	7 36	26 32	18 12	23 57	12 1	22 27	6 52	5 56	15 51

8/23 Sun In Vir. 3:35 8/7 Full 2:41 8/14 3rd Qt. 5:37 8/22 New 9:16 8/29 1st Qt. 19:23

Figure 24 The natal birth date and the progressed birth date

JULY 1960

Day	Sid. T.	Sun	Moon	Merc.	Venus	Mars	Jup.	Saturn	Uranus	Nept.	Pluto	N.Node
·1	18:36:11	9Cn 9 11	25Vi21	29Cn59	11Cn26	7Ta42	27Sg22R	15Cp35R	18Le49	6Sc27R	4Vi 7	19Vi 5
2	18:40: 7	10 6 23	8Li11	0Le 9	12 40	8 25	27 14	15 31	18 53	6 26	4 8	19 2
3	18:44: 4	11 3 35	21 25	0 14	13 54	9 8	27 7	15 26	18 56	6 26	4 10	18 59
4	18:48: 1	12 0 46	5Sc 6	0 14R	15 8	9 50	27 0	15 22	18 59	6 25	4 11	18 56
5	18:51:57	12 57 57	19 16	0 10	16 21	10 33	26 52	15 18	19 2	6 25	4 13	18 53
6	18:55:54	13 55 8	3Sg52	0 1	17 35	11 16	26 45	15 13	19 5	6 24	4 14	18 49
7	18:59:51	14 52 19	18 52	29Cn47	18 49	11 59	26 39	15 9	19 8	6 24	4 15	18 46
8	19: 3:47	15 49 30	4Cp 6	29 29	20 3	12 41	26 32	15 4	19 12	6 24	4 17	18 43
9	19: 7:43	16 46 41	19 24	29 7	21 17	13 23	26 25	15 0	19 15	6 23	4 18	18 40
10	19:11:40	17 43 52	4Aq35	28 41	22 30	14 6	26 18	14 55	19 18	6 23	4 20	18 37
11	19:15:37	18 41 3	19 29	28 11	23 44	14 48	26 12	14 51	19 21	6 23	4 21	18 33
12	19:19:33	19 38 15	4Pi 0	27 39	24 58	15 30	26 5	14 47	19 25	6 23	4 23	18 30
13	19:23:30	20 35 27	18 2	27 3	26 12	16 12	25 59	14 42	19 28	6 22	4 24	18 27
14	19:27:27	21 32 39	1Ar36	26 26	27 26	16 54	25 53	14 38	19 32	6 22	4 26	18 24
15	19:31:23	22 29 53	14 44	25 47	28 39	17 36	25 46	14 34	19 35	6 22	4 28	18 21
16	19:35:20	23 27 6	27 29	25 7	29 53	18 18	25 40	14 29	19 38	6 22	4 29	18 18
17	19:39:16	24 24 21	9Ta56	24 27	1Le 7	19 0	25 34	14 25	19 42	6 22	4 31	18 14
18	19:43:12	25 21 36	22 8	23 47	2 21	19 41	25 29	14 21	19 45	6 22	4 32	18 11
19	19:47: 9	26 18 52	4Ge10	23 9	3 35	20 23	25 23	14 16	19 49	6 22D	4 34	18 8
20	19:51: 6	27 16 8	16 5	22 32	4 49	21 4	25 17	14 12	19 52	6 22	4 36	18 5
21	19:55: 2	28 13 26	27 57	21 58	6 2	21 45	25 12	14 8	19 56	6 22	4 37	18 2
22	19:58:59	29 10 43	9Cn48	21 27	7 16	22 27	25 7	14 4	19 59	6 22	4 39	17 59
23	20: 2:56	0Le 8 2	21 41	21 0	8 30	23 8	25 2	13 59	20 3	6 22	4 41	17 55
24	20: 6:52	1 5 21	3Le36	20 37	9 44	23 49	24 57	13 55	20 7	6 22	4 43	17 52
25	20:10:48	2 2 41	15 36	20 19	10 58	24 30	24 52	13 51	20 10	6 23	4 44	17 49
26	20:14:45	3 0 1	27 42	20 7	12 12	25 10	24 47	13 47	20 14	6 23	4 46	17 46
27	20:18:42	3 57 22	9Vi57	19 59	13 26	25 51	24 43	13 43	20 17	6 23	4 48	17 43
28	20:22:38	4 54 43	22 22	19 58D	14 40	26 32	24 39	13 39	20 21	6 23	4 50	17 39
29	20:26:35	5 52 5	5Li 0	20 2	15 54	27 12	24 34	13 35	20 25	6 24	4 52	17 36
30	20:30:32	6 49 28	17 55	20 13	17 7	27 52	24 30	13 31	20 28	6 24	4 53	17 33
31	20:34:28	7 46 51	1Sc10	20 30	18 21	28 33	24 27	13 27	20 32	6 24	4 55	17 30

7/22 Sun In Leo 20:38 7/2 1st Qt. 3:49 7/8 Full 19:37 7/15 3rd Qt. 15:43 7/23 New 18:31 7/31 1st Qt. 12:39

AUGUST 1960

Day	Sid. T.	Sun	Moon	Merc.	Venus	Mars	Jup.	Saturn	Uranus	Nept.	Pluto	N.Node
1	20:38:24	8Le44 15	14Sc46	20Cn53	19Le35	29Ta13	24Sg23R	13Cp24R	20Le36	6Sc25	4Vi57	17Vi27
2	20:42:21	9 41 39	28 46	21 22	20 49	29 53	24 19	13 20	20 39	6 25	4 59	17 24
3	20:46:17	10 39 4	13Sg 9	21 58	22 3	0Ge33	24 16	13 16	20 43	6 26	5 1	17 20
4	20:50:14	11 36 29	27 52	22 40	23 17	1 12	24 13	13 13	20 47	6 26	5 3	17 17
5	20:54:10	12 33 56	12Cp50	23 28	24 31	1 52	24 10	13 9	20 50	6 27	5 5	17 14
6	20:58: 7	13 31 23	27 54	24 23	25 45	2 31	24 7	13 6	20 54	6 28	5 6	17 11
· 7	21: 2: 4	14 28 51	12Aq55	25 23	26 59	3 11	24 5	13 2	20 58	6 28	5 8	17 8
8	21: 6: 0	15 26 20	27 44	26 [illegible]	28 12	3 50	24 2	12 59	21 1	6 29	5 10	17 5
9	21: 9:57	16 23 50	12Pi14	27 41	29 26	4 29	24 0	12 55	21 5	6 29	5 12	17 1
10	21:13:53	17 21 21	26 20	28 59	0Vi40	5 8	23 58	12 52	21 9	6 30	5 14	16 58
11	21:17:50	18 18 54	10Ar 0	0Le22	1 54	5 47	23 56	12 49	21 13	6 31	5 16	16 55
12	21:21:47	19 16 27	23 13	1 50	3 8	6 25	23 54	12 46	21 16	6 32	5 18	16 52
13	21:25:43	20 14 3	6Ta 3	3 22	4 22	7 4	23 53	12 43	21 20	6 32	5 20	16 49
14	21:29:40	21 11 40	18 32	4 59	5 36	7 42	23 51	12 40	21 24	6 33	5 22	16 45
15	21:33:36	22 9 18	0Ge46	6 40	6 50	8 21	23 50	12 37	21 28	6 34	5 24	16 42
16	21:37:33	23 6 58	12 48	8 25	8 4	8 59	23 49	12 34	21 31	6 35	5 26	16 39
17	21:41:29	24 4 40	24 42	10 13	9 18	9 37	23 48	12 31	21 35	6 36	5 28	16 36
18	21:45:26	25 2 23	6Cn34	12 3	10 32	10 15	23 48	12 29	21 39	6 37	5 30	16 33
19	21:49:22	26 0 8	18 26	13 57	11 45	10 52	23 47	12 26	21 43	6 38	5 32	16 30
20	21:53:19	26 57 54	0Le21	15 52	12 59	11 30	23 47	12 24	21 46	6 39	5 34	16 26
21	21:57:15	27 55 42	12 23	17 49	14 13	12 7	23 47D	12 21	21 50	6 40	5 36	16 23
22	22: 1:12	28 53 31	24 32	19 47	15 27	12 45	23 47	12 19	21 54	6 41	5 38	16 20
23	22: 5: 9	29 51 21	6Vi51	21 46	16 41	13 22	23 48	12 17	21 57	6 42	5 40	16 17
24	22: 9: 5	0Vi49 13	19 21	23 45	17 55	13 59	23 48	12 14	22 1	6 43	5 42	16 14
25	22:13: 2	1 47 6	2Li 3	25 45	19 9	14 35	23 49	12 12	22 5	6 44	5 44	16 11
26	22:16:58	2 45 1	14 58	27 45	20 23	15 12	23 50	12 10	22 8	6 46	5 46	16 7
27	22:20:55	3 42 57	28 7	29 44	21 37	15 48	23 51	12 8	22 12	6 47	5 48	16 4
28	22:24:51	4 40 54	11Sc32	1Vi43	22 51	16 25	23 52	12 6	22 16	6 48	5 50	16 1
29	22:28:48	5 38 53	25 12	3 41	24 5	17 1	23 53	12 5	22 20	6 49	5 52	15 58
30	22:32:45	6 36 53	9Sg 8	5 39	25 18	17 36	23 55	12 3	22 23	6 51	5 54	15 55
31	22:36:41	7 34 55	23 20	7 36	26 32	18 12	23 57	12 1	22 27	6 52	5 56	15 51

8/23 Sun In Vir. 3:35 8/7 Full 2:41 8/14 3rd Qt. 5:37 8/22 New 9:16 8/29 1st Qt. 19:23

Figure 25 Move Venus from 26 to 27 degrees of Leo

AUGUST 1960

Day	Sid. T.	Sun	Moon	Merc.	Venus	Mars	Jup.	Saturn	Uranus	Nept.	Pluto	N.Node
1	20:38:24	8Le44 15	14Sc46	20Cn53	19Le35	29Ta13	24Sg23R	13Cp24R	20Le36	6Sc25	4Vi57	17Vi27
2	20:42:21	9 41 39	28 46	21 22	20 49	29 53	24 19	13 20	20 39	6 25	4 59	17 24
3	20:46:17	10 39 4	13Sg 9	21 58	22 3	0Ge33	24 16	13 16	20 43	6 26	5 1	17 20
4	20:50:14	11 36 29	27 52	22 40	23 17	1 12	24 13	13 13	20 47	6 26	5 3	17 17
5	20:54:10	12 33 56	12Cp50	23 28	24 31	1 52	24 10	13 9	20 50	6 27	5 5	17 14
6	20:58: 7	13 31 23	27 54	24 23	25 45	2 31	24 7	13 6	20 54	6 28	5 6	17 11
· 7	21: 2: 4	14 28 51	12Aq55	25 23	26 59	3 11	24 5	13 2	20 58	6 28	5 8	17 8
8	21: 6: 0	15 26 20	27 44	26 29	28 12	3 50	24 2	12 59	21 1	6 29	5 10	17 5
9	21: 9:57	16 23 50	12Pi14	27 41	29 26	4 29	24 0	12 55	21 5	6 29	5 12	17 1
10	21:13:53	17 21 21	26 20	28 59	0Vi40	5 8	23 58	12 52	21 9	6 30	5 14	16 58
11	21:17:50	18 18 54	10Ar 0	0Le22	1 54	5 47	23 56	12 49	21 13	6 31	5 16	16 55
12	21:21:47	19 16 27	23 13	1 50	3 8	6 25	23 54	12 46	21 16	6 32	5 18	16 52
13	21:25:43	20 14 3	6Ta 3	3 22	4 22	7 4	23 53	12 43	21 20	6 32	5 20	16 49
14	21:29:40	21 11 40	18 32	4 59	5 36	7 42	23 51	12 40	21 24	6 33	5 22	16 45
15	21:33:36	22 9 18	0Ge46	6 40	6 50	8 21	23 50	12 37	21 28	6 34	5 24	16 42
16	21:37:33	23 6 58	12 48	8 25	8 4	8 59	23 49	12 34	21 31	6 35	5 26	16 39
17	21:41:29	24 4 40	24 42	10 13	9 18	9 37	23 48	12 31	21 35	6 36	5 28	16 36
18	21:45:26	25 2 23	6Cn34	12 3	10 32	10 15	23 48	12 29	21 39	6 37	5 30	16 33
19	21:49:22	26 0 8	18 26	13 57	11 45	10 52	23 47	12 26	21 43	6 38	5 32	16 30
20	21:53:19	26 57 54	0Le21	15 52	12 59	11 30	23 47	12 24	21 46	6 39	5 34	16 26
21	21:57:15	27 55 42	12 23	17 49	14 13	12 7	23 47D	12 21	21 50	6 40	5 36	16 23
22	22: 1:12	28 53 31	24 32	19 47	15 27	12 45	23 47	12 19	21 54	6 41	5 38	16 20
23	22: 5: 9	29 51 21	6Vi51	21 46	16 41	13 22	23 48	12 17	21 57	6 42	5 40	16 17
24	22: 9: 5	0Vi49 13	19 21	23 45	17 55	13 59	23 48	12 14	22 1	6 43	5 42	16 14
25	22:13: 2	1 47 6	2Li 3	25 45	19 9	14 35	23 49	12 12	22 5	6 44	5 44	16 11
26	22:16:58	2 45 1	14 58	27 45	20 23	15 12	23 50	12 10	22 8	6 46	5 46	16 7
27	22:20:55	3 42 57	28 7	29 44	21 37	15 48	23 51	12 8	22 12	6 47	5 48	16 4
28	22:24:51	4 40 54	11Sc32	1Vi43	22 51	16 25	23 52	12 6	22 16	6 48	5 50	16 1
29	22:28:48	5 38 53	25 12	3 41	24 5	17 1	23 53	12 5	22 20	6 49	5 52	15 58
30	22:32:45	6 36 53	9Sg 8	5 39	25 18	17 36	23 55	12 3	22 23	6 51	5 54	15 55
31	22:36:41	7 34 55	23 20	7 36	26 32	18 12	23 57	12 1	22 27	6 52	5 56	15 51

8/23 Sun In Vir. 3:35 8/7 Full 2:41 8/14 3rd Qt. 5:37 8/22 New 9:16 8/29 1st Qt. 19:23

Figure 26 ***The Moon needs to be adjusted***

TABLES OF HOUSES FOR LONDON, *Latitude* 51° 32′ N.

H.	M.	S.	10 ♎ °	11 ♎ °	12 ♏ °	Ascen ♐ °	′	2 ♑ °	3 ♒ °
12	0	0	0	27	17	3	23	8	21
12	3	40	1	28	18	4	4	9	23
12	7	20	2	29	19	4	45	10	24
12	11	0	3	♏	20	5	26	11	25
12	14	41	4	1	20	6	7	12	26
12	18	21	5	1	21	6	48	13	27
12	22	2	6	2	22	7	29	14	28
12	25	42	7	3	23	8	10	15	29
12	29	23	8	4	23	8	51	16	♓
12	33	4	9	5	24	9	33	17	2
12	36	45	10	6	25	10	15	18	3
12	40	26	11	6	25	10	57	19	4
12	44	8	12	7	26	11	40	20	5
12	47	50	13	8	27	12	22	21	6
12	51	32	14	9	28	13	4	22	7
12	55	14	15	10	28	13	47	23	9
12	58	57	16	11	29	14	30	24	10
13	2	40	17	11	♐	15	14	25	11
13	6	23	18	12	1	15	59	26	12
13	10	7	19	13	1	16	44	27	13
13	13	51	20	14	2	17	29	28	15
13	17	35	21	15	3	18	14	29	16
13	21	20	22	16	4	19	0	♒	17
13	25	6	23	16	4	19	45	1	18
13	28	52	24	17	5	20	31	2	20
13	32	38	25	18	6	21	18	4	21
13	36	25	26	19	7	22	6	5	22
13	40	12	27	20	7	22	54	6	23
13	44	0	28	21	8	23	42	7	25
13	47	48	29	21	9	24	31	8	26
13	51	37	30	22	10	25	20	10	27

H.	M.	S.	10 ♏ °	11 ♏ °	12 ♐ °	Ascen ♐ °	′	2 ♒ °	3 ♓ °
13	51	37	0	22	10	25	20	10	27
13	55	27	1	23	11	26	10	11	28
13	59	17	2	24	11	27	2	12	♈
14	3	8	3	25	12	27	53	14	1
14	6	59	4	26	13	28	45	15	2
14	10	51	5	26	14	29	36	16	4
14	14	44	6	27	15	0 ♑	29	18	5
14	18	37	7	28	15	1	23	19	6
14	22	31	8	29	16	2	18	20	8
14	26	25	9	♐	17	3	14	22	9
14	30	20	10	1	18	4	11	23	10
14	34	16	11	2	19	5	9	25	11
14	38	13	12	2	20	6	7	26	13
14	42	10	13	3	20	7	6	28	14
14	46	8	14	4	21	8	6	29	15
14	50	7	15	5	22	9	8	♓	17
14	54	7	16	6	23	10	11	2	18
14	58	7	17	7	24	11	15	4	19
15	2	8	18	8	25	12	20	6	21
15	6	9	19	9	26	13	27	8	22
15	10	12	20	9	27	14	35	9	23
15	14	15	21	10	27	15	43	11	24
15	18	19	22	11	28	16	52	13	26
15	22	23	23	12	29	18	3	14	27
15	26	29	24	13	♑	19	16	16	28
15	30	35	25	14	1	20	32	17	29
15	34	41	26	15	2	21	48	19	♉
15	38	49	27	16	3	23	8	21	2
15	42	57	28	17	4	24	29	22	3
15	47	6	29	18	5	25	51	24	5
15	51	15	30	18	6	27	15	26	6

H.	M.	S.	10 ♐ °	11 ♐ °	12 ♑ °	Ascen ♑ °	′	2 ♓ °	3 ♉ °
15	51	15	0	18	6	27	15	26	6
15	55	25	1	19	7	28	42	28	7
15	59	36	2	20	8	0 ♒	11	♈	9
16	3	48	3	21	9	1	42	2	10
16	8	0	4	22	10	3	16	3	11
16	12	13	5	23	11	4	53	5	12
16	16	26	6	24	12	6	32	7	14
16	20	40	7	25	13	8	13	9	15
16	24	55	8	26	14	9	57	11	16
16	29	10	9	27	16	11	44	12	17
16	33	26	10	28	17	13	34	14	18
16	37	42	11	29	18	15	26	16	20
16	41	59	12	♑	19	17	20	18	21
16	46	16	13	1	20	19	18	20	22
16	50	34	14	2	21	21	22	21	23
16	54	52	15	3	22	23	29	23	25
16	59	10	16	4	24	25	36	25	26
17	3	29	17	5	25	27	46	27	27
17	7	49	18	6	26	0 ♓	0	28	28
17	12	9	19	7	27	2	19	♉	29
17	16	29	20	8	29	4	40	2	♊
17	20	49	21	9	♒	7	2	3	1
17	25	9	22	10	1	9	26	5	2
17	29	30	23	11	3	11	54	7	3
17	33	51	24	12	4	14	24	8	5
17	38	12	25	13	5	17	0	10	6
17	42	34	26	14	7	19	33	11	7
17	46	55	27	15	8	22	6	13	8
17	51	17	28	16	10	24	40	14	9
17	55	38	29	17	11	27	20	16	10
18	0	0	30	18	13	30	0	17	11

H.	M.	S.	10 ♑ °	11 ♑ °	12 ♒ °	Ascen ♈ °	′	2 ♉ °	3 ♊ °
18	0	0	0	18	13	0	0	17	11
18	4	22	1	20	14	2	39	18	13
18	8	43	2	21	16	5	19	20	14
18	13	5	3	22	17	7	55	22	15
18	17	26	4	23	19	10	29	23	16
18	21	48	5	24	20	13	2	25	17
18	26	9	6	25	22	15	36	26	18
18	30	30	7	26	23	18	6	28	19
18	34	51	8	27	25	20	34	29	20
18	39	11	9	29	27	22	59	♊	21
18	43	31	10	♒	28	25	22	1	22
18	47	51	11	1	♓	27	42	2	23
18	52	11	12	2	2	29	58	4	24
18	56	31	13	3	3	2 ♉	13	5	25
19	0	50	14	4	5	4	24	6	26
19	5	8	15	6	7	6	30	8	27
19	9	26	16	7	9	8	36	9	28
19	13	44	17	8	10	10	40	10	29
19	18	1	18	9	12	12	39	11	♋
19	22	18	19	10	14	14	35	12	1
19	26	34	20	12	16	16	28	13	2
19	30	50	21	13	18	18	17	14	3
19	35	5	22	14	19	20	3	16	4
19	39	20	23	15	21	21	48	17	5
19	43	34	24	16	23	23	29	18	6
19	47	47	25	18	25	25	9	19	7
19	52	0	26	19	27	26	45	20	8
19	56	12	27	20	28	28	18	21	9
20	0	24	28	21	♈	29	49	22	10
20	4	35	29	23	2	1 ♊	19	23	11
20	8	45	30	24	4	2	45	24	12

H.	M.	S.	10 ♒ °	11 ♒ °	12 ♈ °	Ascen ♊ °	′	2 ♊ °	3 ♋ °
20	8	45	0	24	4	2	45	24	12
20	12	54	1	25	6	4	9	25	12
20	17	3	2	27	7	5	32	26	13
20	21	11	3	28	9	6	53	27	14
20	25	19	4	29	11	8	12	28	15
20	29	26	5	♓	13	9	27	29	16
20	33	31	6	2	14	10	43	♋	17
20	37	37	7	3	16	11	58	1	18
20	41	41	8	4	18	13	9	2	19
20	45	45	9	6	19	14	18	3	20
20	49	48	10	7	21	15	25	3	21
20	53	51	11	8	23	16	32	4	21
20	57	52	12	9	24	17	39	5	22
21	1	53	13	11	26	18	44	6	23
21	5	53	14	12	28	19	48	7	24
21	9	53	15	13	29	20	51	8	25
21	13	52	16	15	♉	21	53	9	26
21	17	50	17	16	2	22	53	10	27
21	21	47	18	17	4	23	52	10	28
21	25	44	19	19	5	24	51	11	28
21	29	40	20	20	7	25	48	12	29
21	33	35	21	22	8	26	44	13	♌
21	37	29	22	23	10	27	40	14	1
21	41	23	23	24	11	28	34	15	2
21	45	16	24	25	13	29	29	15	3
21	49	9	25	26	14	0 ♋	22	16	4
21	53	1	26	28	15	1	15	17	4
21	56	52	27	29	16	2	7	18	5
22	0	43	28	♈	18	2	57	19	6
22	4	33	29	2	19	3	48	19	7
22	8	23	30	3	20	4	38	20	8

H.	M.	S.	10 ♓ °	11 ♈ °	12 ♉ °	Ascen ♋ °	′	2 ♋ °	3 ♌ °
22	8	23	0	3	20	4	38	20	8
22	12	12	1	4	21	5	28	21	8
22	16	0	2	6	23	6	17	22	9
22	19	48	3	7	24	7	5	23	10
22	23	35	4	8	25	7	53	23	11
22	27	22	5	9	26	8	42	24	12
22	31	8	6	10	28	9	29	25	13
22	34	54	7	12	29	10	16	26	14
22	38	40	8	13	♊	11	2	26	14
22	42	25	9	14	1	11	47	27	15
22	46	9	10	15	2	12	31	28	16
22	49	53	11	17	3	13	16	29	17
22	53	37	12	18	4	14	1	29	18
22	57	20	13	19	5	14	45	♌	19
23	1	3	14	20	6	15	28	1	19
23	4	46	15	21	7	16	11	2	20
23	8	28	16	23	8	16	54	2	21
23	12	10	17	24	9	17	37	3	22
23	15	52	18	25	10	18	20	4	23
23	19	34	19	26	11	19	3	5	24
23	23	15	20	27	12	19	45	5	24
23	26	56	21	29	13	20	26	6	25
23	30	37	22	♉	14	21	8	7	26
23	34	18	23	1	15	21	50	7	27
23	37	58	24	2	16	22	31	8	28
23	41	39	25	3	17	23	12	9	28
23	45	19	26	4	18	23	53	9	29
23	49	0	27	5	19	24	32	10	♍
23	52	40	28	6	20	25	15	11	1
23	56	20	29	8	21	25	56	12	2
24	0	0	30	9	22	26	36	13	3

Figure 27 ***The new midheaven is shown to be 2 degrees of Capricorn and the new ascendant at 5 degrees of Aries (from*** **Raphael's Astronomical Ephemeris)**

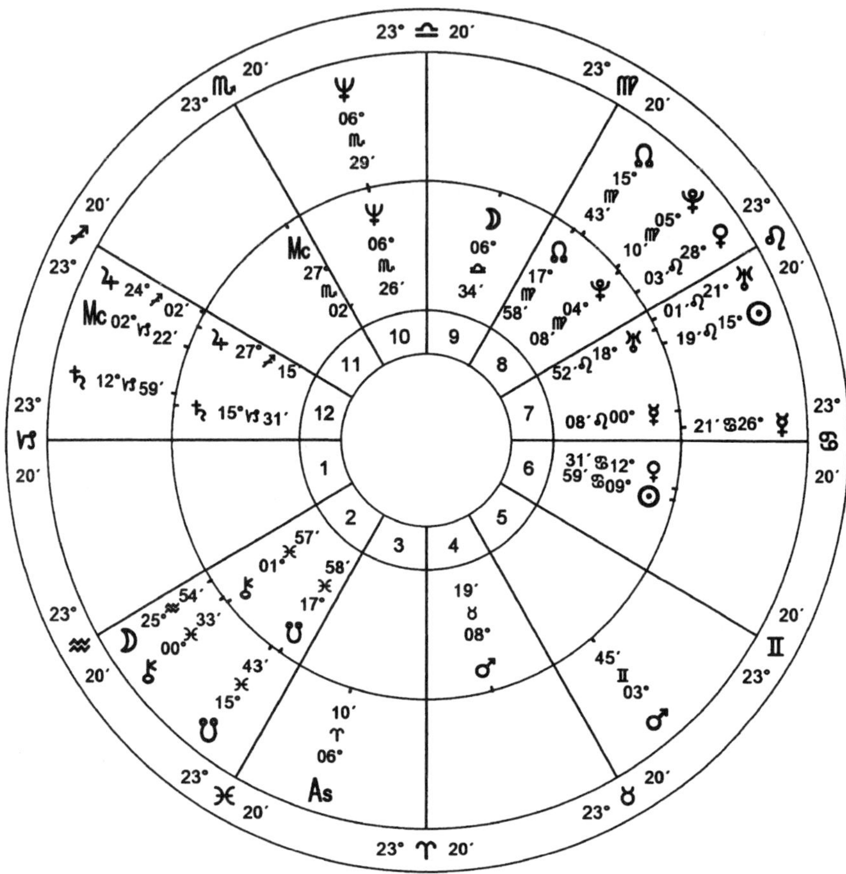

Figure 28 A Natal and Progressed Chart
The inner wheel shows the natal chart and the outer wheel the progressed chart

9. Now, count down the midheaven column a day for each year of life. There is one slightly awkward thing to bear in mind. The ephemeris will show midheaven positions as going from 0 degrees of a sign to 30 degrees, whereas we use only 29 degrees of a sign. Count *everything* including the zero and the 30 (see figure 27).
10. Now look across the column to find the new ascendant (in the same way that you found the natal one). There are a variety of ways of calculating a progressed ascendant, and,

while this method may not be a hundred per cent accurate, it will do well enough for now.

11. If your subject has moved from one part of the world to another, you may want to calculate the progressed chart for the new location rather than for the place where they were born.
12. If you really don't fancy making these calculations, USE A COMPUTER!!!

Comparison of hand-generated figures with computerized ones

The first column below shows hand-worked progressions, while the second column has been computer generated. When compared with the hand-generated table, the first thing that becomes obvious is that the computer gives the degrees and minutes, while the rough and ready hand chart gives only whole degrees.

Hand Chart		***Computer Chart***	
Sun:	15 Leo	Sun:	15.19 Leo
Moon:	25 Aquarius	Moon:	25.54 Aquarius
Mercury:	26 Cancer	Mercury:	26.21 Cancer
Venus:	27 (28) Leo	Venus:	28.04 Leo
Mars:	3 Gemini	Mars:	3.46 Gemini
Jupiter:	24 Sagittarius	Jupiter:	24.02 Sagittarius
Saturn:	13 (12) Capricorn	Saturn:	12.59 Capricorn
Uranus:	21 Leo	Uranus:	21.01 Leo
Neptune:	6 Scorpio	Neptune:	6.29 Scorpio
Pluto:	5 Virgo	Pluto:	5.11 Virgo
North Node:	17 Virgo	True Node:	15.43 Virgo
Asc:	5 Aries	Asc:	3.04 Aries
MC:	2 Capricorn	MC:	1.10 Capricorn

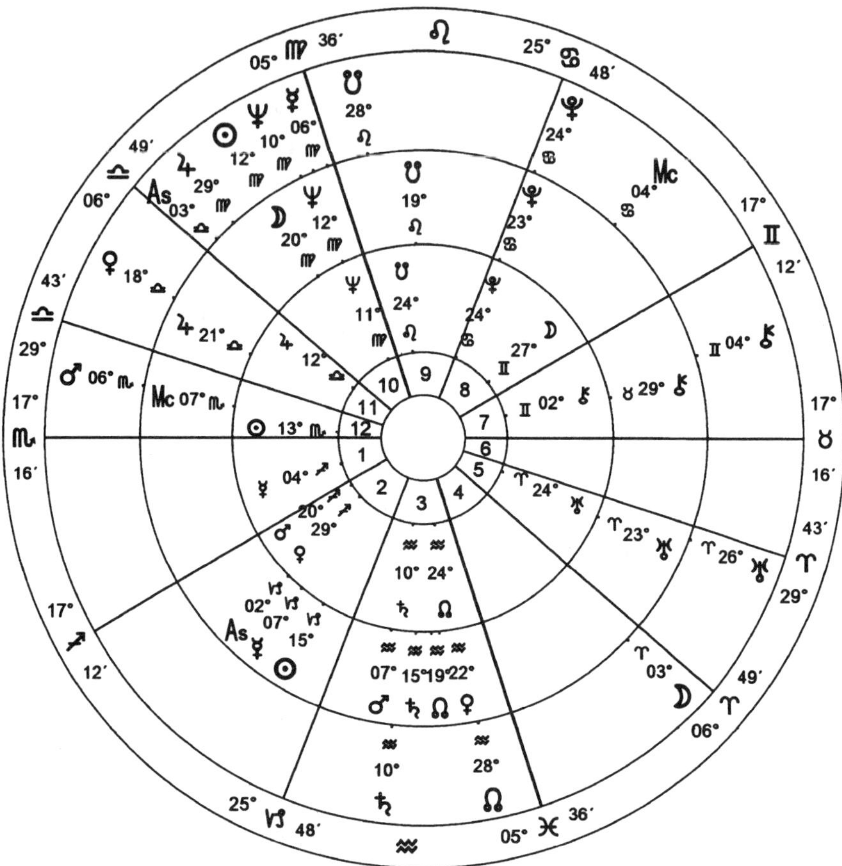

Figure 29 Tony Fenton – Natal, Progressed and Transit Charts
The inner wheel shows the natal chart, the middle wheel the progressed chart, and the outer wheel the transit chart

Inner Wheel	Middle Wheel	Outer Wheel
Tony Fenton	**Tony Fenton**	**Tony Fenton**
Natal Chart	**Sec.Prog. Q2 SA**	**Sec.Prog. Q2 SA**
Nov 6 1933	**in Long**	**in Long**
07:30 GMT +0:00	Apr 26 1995	**Converse**
London	13:15 GMT +0:00	Apr 26 1995
51N30 000W10	London	13:15 GMT +0:00
	51N30 000W10	London
		51N30 000W10

Having gone through this exercise, I am surprised at how well the hand-generated chart compares with the computerized one. I expected the ascendant and the midheaven to be much further out of true than they were, and the planetary positions are not bad at all. However, the north node of the Moon is out by over a degree. This is because the ephemeris shows the north node, while the program that I used showed the true node. This slight difference is not too critical and you can choose to use either.

The whole chart

Figure 28 is a computer version of the whole thing, with the natal chart on the inner ring and the progressed positions on the middle one, with the *natal* ascendant and houses shown on the outer ring.

Wheels within wheels

Despite the fact that computerized charts are lovely and clear, in my opinion this kind of triple wheel is too much to handle at one time. It is best to make up a bi-wheel with the natal chart on the inside and the progressed one on the outside. If transits are also wanted, simply look at the ephemeris or list the transits on a separate page. Figure 29 shows how confusing a triple chart can be.

11

All the other Progressions

THE ONLY FORMS of predictive astrology that I am covering in detail in this book are the four methods that have already been mentioned: solar returns, lunar returns, solar arc progressions and day-for-a-year progressions. However, I would like to demystify some of the amazing terminology that is used to describe various forms of chart manipulation. In many cases the variety of terms are simply different names for the same old methods. The following list covers most of the terms that you are likely to come across, and I will now go into all of them in a kind of *Which?* report, with an honest opinion as to their usefulness or otherwise. You will soon see that none of this is as daunting as it looks.

The horrendous list of terms

Progressions
Day-for-a-year progressions
Secondary directions
Secondary progressions
Primary directions
Solar arc directions
Solar arc progressions
Solar arc MC progressions
One degree progressions
Tertiary progressions
Minor progressions
Daily house progressions
Duodenary progressions
Converse directions
Converse progressions
90 degree arc
Solar returns
Solar return directions
Lunar returns
Venusian arcs
Martial arcs
Decumbitures
Hororary astrology
Electional astrology
Mundane astrology

Progressions

This name simply covers any method of progressing a horoscope – that is, anything that moves a chart by some form of mathematical calculation. If an astrologer talks about progressions or a progressed horoscope, the chances are that he is talking about the most popular method of them all – the day-for-a-year method.

Converse progressions, directions, etc.

All methods of progression can be done *BACKWARDS as well as forwards!* I first came across this idea many years ago in a book by the late Ronald Davison. I tried it out with both the day-for-a-year and the solar arc methods, and I found that it did turn up a few things that didn't otherwise show. However, it was so awkward to do by hand that I gave up after one or two tries. Modern computer programs will happily provide converse progressions if you should want them, so enthusiastic student astrologers should have a go at one or two of these in order to satisfy their curiosity. My own curiosity will probably remain dormant as far as this method is concerned.

Day-for-a-year progressions, secondary progressions, secondary directions, solar arc MC progressions

All these terms mean exactly the same thing! In this book I have decided to use the name that is most commonly understood in the United Kingdom, day-for-a-year progressions. You will find this described in detail in Chapter 10.

Most astrologers simply refer to the day-for-a-year method as 'progressions', because this is the most popular form of astrological progression. This is not difficult to do by hand and it is available on every astrological computer program. The problem here is that computer programs are usually American in origin and American astrologers tend to make up their own names for everything!

Solar arc directions, primary directions, one degree progressions, solar arc directed charts

Once again, all these terms mean much the same thing. Call them solar arc progressions.

This is truly easy to do by hand and absolutely instantaneous when done by a computer. All you do is to take each planet and move it one degree for each year of life. Technically speaking, there *is* a slight difference between the different terms because the one-degree progressions simply move everything forward by one degree, while the other methods may move the chart forward by the same amount in each year as the daily motion of either the midheaven or the Sun. If you need to be accurate, use a computer.

As an astrologer, I find the solar arc technique a bit crude, because it doesn't take account of the difference in speed at which each of the planets moves, and it ignores the possibility of retrograde motion. However, it is worth progressing the Sun and the midheaven by this method and taking a look at what shows up.

A *useful tip*

Progressing the midheaven one degree per year can be a very handy tool when trying to rectify a chart in order to work out exactly when someone was born. I will describe this technique for you at the end of this chapter since, although technically speaking it has nothing to do with predictive astrology, I am including it because you are bound to find it useful. This will work when the subject has some idea of his birth time. Other methods need to be used if there is no clue at all about the time of birth.

Tertiary progressions

This moves the chart by one day for a lunar month (27.32 days). You can't do this without a computer but if you give it a try you will find it interesting. It is fun to play about with but not worth using seriously.

Minor progressions

This method substitutes a lunar month (27.32 days) for a year. It is also interesting but you cannot even think about doing it without a computer. Like the tertiary progressions, this one is not worth spending too much time or energy on.

Duodenary progressions

Divide each sign by 12 divisions of two-and-a-half degrees each. Progress each planet and angle by one two-and-a-half segment for each year of life. I vaguely remember trying this out when I was in the early stages of discovering astrology but I have never used it for a client. It is based on the 'Lunar mansions'.

90-degree arc

I have tried manfully to understand this one but, so far, no luck. The idea (I think) is to break the chart down into its component elements of fire, earth, air and water, then put all the fire segments together and progress them, doing the same for all the other element 'blocks' in turn. I know that modern computer programs offer this method as an option, but how it works and what use it may be still eludes me!

Solar returns, solar return directions

This method is described in detail in Chapter 8. I have used this technique on clients' charts many times over the years, and I consider it to be the second most useful of all the predictive techniques. Sometimes it is more informative than even the day-for-a-year method.

This is very tricky to work out by hand but is very easily accomplished on a computer. The idea is to place the Sun in the exact degree and minute that it was at the moment of birth and then array all the other planets, in addition to the ascendant, midheaven and everything else, around it for that moment in time. This is actually a *transit* chart for the anniversary of the moment of birth in any year. When glanced at quickly, solar returns seem to offer a flavour of what the year ahead will bring, and the ascendant in particular gives a strong picture of what the coming year will feel like. However, when looked at methodically, a solar return chart can be very revealing indeed.

A *useful tip*

In the case of the majority of the predictive methods, you will get the best results by putting your progressed or transit chart around or against a natal chart and seeing how the new planetary positions affect the original ones. The solar and lunar return charts are different, in that they seem to work best when looked at *in their own right* without being placed against any other kind of chart. Try this as a stand-alone chart and also try it out against the natal chart; I think you will find that the stand-alone method works much better and is far less confusing.

Lunar returns

This is similar to the solar return, and it is a very handy way of focusing on a very short period of time rather than a long-term trend. It is so useful that I have described it fully in Chapter 8.

The idea is to place the Moon at the exact degree and minute that was on the natal chart and then array the rest of the chart around this new position, with the ascendant and midheaven, etc., all carefully recalculated. This is obviously a job for a computer and it offers a flavour of the month in question.

A *useful tip*

When looking at a lunar return, bear in mind that the subject's mood and the events seem to come into operation a week or so before the actual date of the return and then begin to fade away a couple of weeks afterwards. Also, I suggest that you look at this chart in its own right as a stand-alone chart without putting it against the natal chart.

Venusian arcs and martian arcs

The idea here is similar to solar arc directions, that is, to move the whole chart by the amount that either Venus or Mars would have travelled during the course of a number of years. As both of these planets appear to move at varying speeds and also change from forward motion into retrograde motion and back again from time to time, this is obviously one for an Einstein to play with. I don't even know of a computer program that can tackle this. Forget it!

Decumbitures

This is an absolutely fascinating area of astrology, and it is used to diagnose and plot the history of an illness. This is associated with the ancient medical ideas of the 'humours' and was used years ago by the herbalist Nicholas Culpeper and the astrologer William Lilly. A few specialists in the more ancient forms of astrology and also herbal medicines still use this method, the most noteworthy modern proponent being Dylan Warren-Davis. Decumbitures follow ancient and specialized rules.

Horary astrology

This is an ancient method of prediction that has recently come back into favour. It is based on the idea that one makes up a chart for the *moment* that a question is asked and then the chart is assessed in order to find the answer. This can be done by following normal astrological systems, but true horary astrology has rules of its own. This takes a lot of study before one can become competent. Look at the further reading list at the end of this volume for a good book on this subject.

Sasha's 'hororary for beginners' method

Simply set up a chart for the time that you first embarked on a course of action or for the moment when you ask a particular question and then interpret it as you would for a person or a situation. Use the usual rules for natal charting but add a touch of intuition to your reading. Don't forget to use house rulers to see what the situation is all about. For example, I recently set out to do something creative with a partner, and in the hororary chart for the start of the venture, both the seventh and eighth housc (on a Placidus chart system) were ruled by Pisces. This venture never even got off the ground!

Electional astrology

This is, in a way, a reverse form of predictive astrology, because the idea is to pick the right *moment* to act upon something that has already been decided upon. This is typically used in India and throughout the East in order to select the day and time for a marriage or for the start of an important enterprise. What the astrologer is trying to do here is to give the marriage or enterprise the best possible chance of success, not just on the day it starts, but over a period of time. While writing this, my friends Denise and Mike have decided to get married. They asked me to select the best date and time for their wedding.

The British Astrological and Psychic Society always asks one of its astrologers to find the best possible day and time, within the limits that are possible, for its annual general meetings. Many astrologers, including me, use this method for choosing the right time to do something important.

Mundane astrology

The term *mundane* in this case means 'of the world', and it is exactly like any other form of astrology, except that it refers to the fortunes of cities, countries, political parties or any other kind of organization. Mundane astrology involves making up a natal chart to show the character of the organization, town or country in question. All the usual predictive techniques can be used against this natal chart. If you want to work for any form of the media, this is probably the most important of all forms of astrology. If you have even the slightest intention of looking into this method, you will need to get the two books that Nick Campion has written. The first, *Mundane Astrology*, tells you how to do it and the second, *The Book of World Horoscopes* is absolutely invaluable to any professional astrologer.

Daily house progressions

I found this on my latest computer program, but it is not clear to me just what it is! The program manual doesn't give much of a clue either. The planets appear to be progressed by the usual day-for-a-year method but the ascendant and houses are different.

Perpetual noon date

This method is supposed to be a much more accurate version of the day-for-a-year method. The only place in which I have ever seen it explained in full is *Parker's Astrology* by Derek and Julia Parker. It is extremely long-winded and difficult to do by hand and, after a bit of initial experimentation, I have never bothered to use it. It is a pity that such a comprehensive book includes only this method of progression.

During my first ten years or so as an astrologer all my work had to be done by hand, and, as my clients rarely had a clear idea of the time of their births, I considered that accuracy on this level wasn't worth striving for. If you are going to become a professional astrologer, you will soon get used to adjusting charts as you go in order to get the timing right. The next item shows you how to rectify a slightly 'dodgy' chart by hand. Computer programs are accurate, of course, and nowadays they have a rectification procedure built into them.

Using the midheaven for rectification

As promised earlier in this chapter, here is a useful aid to working out the exact time of a person's birth, but it will only work if the subject has some idea of when they were born. Take the earliest and the latest times at which the subject thinks they may have been born and make up a chart for the middle of these. Then ask your subject to pick an incident out of their childhood for you to use as a 'hook' on which to hang the chart. An obvious one would be the date on which they started school, particularly if this was traumatic in any way. Other ideas would be of a childhood accident, a move of house or anything else that stands out in your subject's mind. Now, move the midheaven forward by a degree for a year and see if it makes any aspect to any appropriate planet or any other hot spot (such as an angle) at the age that it is supposed to. If it does, then take another incident and try again. If you get the timing on at least two events right, you have found the correct time of birth. If the events seem to come about a little before or after the midheaven transit, then your birth time is out one way or the other and can be easily adjusted. This is not difficult to do by hand and it is very easy on a modern computer program which is equipped with a rectification facility.

Bear in mind that an appropriate planet for a child having an accident could be Mars or the planet that rules the part of the body that was hurt. A broken leg, for example, would be a Jupiter, Saturn or Uranus matter. A move of house or a family problem would involve the Moon, while happiness or unhappiness at school would suggest a Mercury situation. An ailment would connect with whatever planet ruled the part of the body that was involved: for example, jaundice – Jupiter, tonsils – Venus. Also watch for the signs and houses in which any events occur. A certain amount of intuition and also some blind faith can be a great help when solving this form of astrological conundrum.

12

A Recap: the Right Method for Each Job

THE PREVIOUS chapter was designed to show you what the various forms of progression are and how they work. This one is intended to show you which type of technique to choose, and for what purpose.

Transits

Use transits when you want to take a quick glance at a chart. Transits can be used to look at any aspect of life (love, health, work, etc.). They are also useful when you want to focus on a specific period of time, such as a particular few days.

Day-for-a-year progressions

This method gives a good overview of a subject's situation and it also gives plenty of specific information. The Moon is the thing to watch, because it shows the general mood and outlook of the subject at the time of the reading and it moves quickly enough by progression for an astrologer to pick out special events. Do the progressions and then use the transits against both the natal and progressed charts for the very best results.

Solar arc directions

This is useful for a general look at a subject's life. If nothing else, try looking at the progressed midheaven and the progressed Sun. I have never used transits against this method but there is no reason why you shouldn't.

Tertiary, minor and duodenary progressions and 90-degree arc

Experiment with these if you like. I've never used them commercially.

Solar and lunar returns

These are extremely useful, especially the solar returns. If you don't get a great result by other methods, try these. The solar returns can be used to focus on a particular situation, or on life in general, and lunar returns to give an even closer look.

Venusian and martian arcs

Leave these on Venus and Mars!

Decumbitures

If you like horary astrology, you will love decumbitures. Use them to analyse and diagnose an illness. This is a great aid to astrological herbalists and the like. You need to be fully conversant with all aspects of decumbitures before diagnosing anything.

Horary astrology

Ask yourself a question, such as, 'Will I get the job I want?' Make up a chart for the time the question is asked and see if it answers it. This is best for those who have thoroughly studied this technique.

Electional astrology

Make up your mind to do something and then find the best time for it. Try making up a chart of the time and date you think is right as if it were a natal chart, and then looking at its chances of success.

Mundane astrology

Try finding the chart for a specific country or a political party and work out what is likely to happen to it over the next six months.

13

Aspects between the Progressed/Transit and the Natal Chart

THE NORMAL TYPE of day-for-a-year progressions can be made into a separate stand-alone chart which can be looked at in its own right. However, the best way to use these is to put the progressions around the natal chart, either by hand or on your computer, and then look at the aspects that are formed between the two charts. If you are used to looking at planets that transit a natal chart, use the same method and the same interpretations for what you find. Luckily, any book that offers interpretations of the transits can be used for the progressions as well. Solar arc charts should be used in exactly the same way, by looking at them against the natal chart. However, solar and lunar returns are probably best taken as stand-alone charts, but there is no reason why you shouldn't try both methods and make up your own mind about their efficacy. Such things as electional charts, and any kind of chart that is erected for the time that a question is asked or for the moment when something starts, can be looked at only as stand-alone charts.

If you find it confusing to contemplate two sets of planets on one chart, then list your progressions and compare each planet to the natal chart in turn. If you have a good computer program, make up a bi-wheel chart, a list of natal planets and also a list of the progressions (or transits) to the natal planets.

Aspects

Once you have everything in place, you need to know what the aspects are and what they mean. Progressed or transiting aspects work in the same way as natal aspects and the terminology is the same for both. The difference is that a natal aspect will show you something about the *character* of your subject, while the mobile ones show *trends* and *events*.

Astrologers are violently allergic to the terms 'good' and 'bad', so 'good' aspects are often referred to as being *easy* or *beneficial*, while 'bad' ones are often called *challenging*. This kind of astrological political correctness may be irritating but there is a reason for it. Nothing in astrology is truly black and white and no planet or aspect can be considered to be really *bad*, while any aspect, however beneficial, can have some strangely unpleasant side effects. The trick is to take into account the energies behind each planet and the modifying effects of the signs and houses that are emphasized. This sounds complicated but I can assure you that it soon becomes second nature.

Orbs

Question: When is an aspect not an aspect?
Answer: When it is out of orb.

A conjunction occurs when two planets are in the same place – for example, when natal Saturn is at 13 degrees of Taurus and transiting Venus passes over the same spot. However, that conjunction can be in operation for up to eight degrees either side of the actual point of contact. This is called the *allowable orb*. Astrologers have slightly different opinions as to the size of the orbs, so there are no hard and fast rules to be obeyed. It is worth bearing in mind that an aspect can often be felt coming for a long time before it actually connects on a chart and its effects can fizzle out quite quickly once it has arrived. When a planet does a retrograde dance backwards and forwards over a sensitive point on a chart its effects can be felt for months or even years until it finally passes away from the trouble spot.

The table of aspects

The table of aspects laid out below lists all the major ones and most of the minor ones as well.

The Table of Aspects

Symbol	*Aspect*	*Distance between*	*Allowable orb*
☌	Conjunction	0 degrees	8 degrees
☍	Opposition	180 degrees	8 degrees
△	Trine	120 degrees	8 degrees
□	Square	90 degrees	8 degrees
⚹	Sextile	60 degrees	6 degrees
∠	Semi-square	45 degrees	2 degrees
⚼	Sesquiquadrate	135 degrees	2 degrees
⚻	Inconjunct or quincunx	150 degrees	2 degrees
⚺	Semi-sextile	30 degrees	2 degrees
Q	Quintile	72 degrees	2 degrees
BQ	Bi-quintile	144 degrees	2 degrees

When looking at aspects to the nodes of the Moon or to the part of fortune, then an orb of a degree or so is sufficient.

As in natal charting, the major aspects of conjunction, opposition, trine, square and sextile, along with the inconjunct, are the ones you will use most.

How to read the aspects

The major aspects

Conjunction ☌ 0°

This extremely powerful aspect can register a wonderful event or a pretty nasty one, depending upon the planets that are involved. You must also take into account the signs and houses in which the conjunction occurs, and that a conjunction in one place in a chart means that something else is being opposed, even if this is only a particular sign and house.

There is a *first house* feeling to a conjunction, so, whatever else it does, it always engages the attention of the subject in a very important way. It is also worth noting that the outcome of the conjunction often works out well in the long run or that something good comes out of even the most difficult situation where conjunctions are concerned.

Opposition ☍ 180°

This is considered to be a difficult aspect but I feel that it is where a subject has to deal with or, perhaps, put up with the decisions and the behaviour of others. This doesn't have to be all bad. For example, if a subject is lonely, the movement of planets into opposition to their ascendant or to some of the planets brings new contacts and connections. It is also worth remembering that planets in opposition will be enhancing the sign and house through which they are passing.

There is always a kind of *seventh house* feeling to oppositions and they can be quite fortunate in the long run.

Trine △ 120°

This is always a pleasant, easy and rather lucky aspect, and the worst that can happen is that it is so easy that it goes unnoticed. A trine will set off a period of creativity, love and fun which is in line with the *fifth house* feeling to which it relates. Alternatively, it can bring freedom, the chance of exploring new horizons or of learning something new in a *ninth house* manner.

Square □ 90°

This is probably the most challenging of all aspects. In a natal chart, a square is considered to be character building – that is, if you enjoy a bit of hardship. In a progressed chart, the character-building aspects of this can make the subject extremely unhappy. I don't know what kind of feeling there is attached to this one: probably a *tenth house* feeling of struggle, learning the hard way and determination to overcome problems – maybe even a *fourth house* feeling of going back to the root of a problem and sorting it out from the ground upwards.

Sextile ⚹ 60°

This is another pleasant aspect which brings luck and

happiness. It is supposed to be more mental and *third house* in character than the trine. Therefore one would expect pleasant news or ease of communication related to the planets, signs and houses that are affected by it. This can also bring friendship, group activity, education and exploration of an *eleventh house* kind.

The minor aspects

Semi-square ∠ 45°

This can be quite a difficult aspect, rather like the square but less important. It is hard to spot on a chart without a list of the aspects.

Sesquiquadrate ⚼ 135°

This can be trying. It is a fairly mild aspect.

In conjunct or quincunx ⚻ 150°

Although this is a minor aspect it is always worth considering, both in natal charting and when looking at progressions and transits. It can be extremely awkward and it puts pressure on the subject either in a kind of *sixth house* manner by loading them down with duties and obligations or an *eighth house* manner by landing them with financial, sexual or relationship problems. The two signs involved have nothing in common because they will be of a different element and quality. Two inconjuncts at the same time form what is known as a 'yod' aspect, and this can be very awkward indeed while it lasts.

Semi-sextile ⚺ 30°

Some astrologers see this as being a pleasant aspect, rather like a minor sextile, but I'm not so sure, because the signs that are involved are never compatible with each other. Either way, the events involved are likely to be pretty unremarkable.

Quintile Q 72°

In a natal chart, a quintile aspect is supposed to bestow talent, so I guess that a progressed quintile would bring talents to the fore. This is hard to spot and rarely used.

Bi-quintile BQ 144°
This is much the same as the quintile, but weaker.

Longitudinal and latitudinal aspects

Until very recently, all that the vast majority of astrologers considered were the *longitudinal aspects*. This means that, from our point of view on the Earth, we look at their placement round the Earth against the background of the stars that pass over us. The band of stars that appears to pass around the Earth is called *the ecliptic*, and this is divided into the 12 sections that we know as the signs of the zodiac. Just as the meridian lines of longitude run through the Earth from north to south, the ecliptic is measured in the same way with 360 vertical lines, and it is the planets' positions along this that we measure for aspects. Thus, if one planet is at 2 degrees of Aries and another is 90 degrees away at 2 degrees of Cancer, these planets will be in *square* aspect to each other.

Now see if you can get your head around the concept of parallel and contra-parallel aspects. In the case of a parallel aspect, it doesn't matter where the two planets are along the ecliptic *as long as they are at the same height (latitude) above (or below) the celestial equator*. In a contra-parallel aspect, the two planets would be at the same degree as each other but *one would be above the celestial equator and the other would be below it.* The only ephemeris up to now to show parallel and contra-parallel aspects is *Raphael's Ephemeris*, which comes out each year. However, nowadays modern computer programs show parallels in their lists of aspects. When it comes to interpreting both parallels and contra-parallels, consider them in the same way that you would a conjunction. Indeed, old-time astrologers reckoned that a parallel was a stronger force than a conjunction.

I suggest that if you are in the process of learning your astrology, concentrate on the ordinary major aspects such as the conjunction, sextile, square, trine and opposition first and worry about the more esoteric forms of aspect later on.

14

Further Techniques

IN THIS CHAPTER I gather together a number of ideas that are either very old or very new. Astrologers are taking much more notice of slightly off-beat techniques nowadays and as you progress in your astrological studies, you may want to try some of these for yourself.

Dignity, exaltation, detriment and fall

Planet	*Dignity*	*Exaltation*
Sun	Leo	Aries
Moon	Cancer	Taurus
Mercury	Gemini + Virgo	Virgo
Venus	Taurus + Libra	Pisces
Mars	Aries + Scorpio	Cancer
Jupiter	Sagittarius + Pisces	Capricorn
Saturn	Capricorn + Aquarius	Libra
Planet	***Fall***	***Detriment***
Sun	Libra	Aquarius
Moon	Scorpio	Capricorn
Mercury	Pisces	Sagittarius + Pisces
Venus	Virgo	Scorpio + Aries
Mars	Cancer	Libra + Taurus
Jupiter	Capricorn	Gemini + Virgo
Saturn	Aries	Cancer + Leo

Dignity and exaltation

Planets are said to be comfortable and able to work harmoniously when they are *dignified* or, in other words, in the signs that they rule. Planets are also said to work well when *exalted* (ie comfortable in that sign). Such a planetary placement may help to offset a difficult *aspect*.

Fall and detriment

Planets are less able to work harmoniously in a chart if they are in *fall* or *detriment*. If a planet is well aspected natally but is in fall or detriment, the two situations will help to balance each other out but if a planet is in fall or detriment and is also badly aspected, it makes the situation worse. The following snippet will give you an absolutely up-to-the-minute example. At the very moment of writing this, I have laryngitis – which is something that I am prone to. Venus rules the throat and my own personal Venus is in its fall in Virgo and squared by Saturn and the ascendant.

Houses

The planets are connected to the houses in the same way that they rule the signs.

Planet	***House***
Sun	Fifth
Moon	Fourth
Mercury	Third and sixth
Venus	Second and seventh
Mars	First (also in the past, the eighth)
Jupiter	Ninth (also in the past, the twelfth)
Saturn	Tenth (also in the past, the eleventh)
Uranus	Eleventh
Neptune	Twelfth
Pluto	Eighth

The theory is that a planet is likely to be more effective if in the house that it rules. The problem here is that different house systems can move planets from one house to another. Thus a person with the Moon in the eleventh house on some systems could have it in the twelfth in others. However, the *Gauquelin* system of giving importance to planets that are close to the angles definitely *does* work.

These ancient types of *planetary weighting*, play an important role in horary and other older types of astrology.

Midpoints

Midpoints are the halfway point between two planets, or between a planet and an angle, or between two angles. Progressions or transits to an important midpoint can be as effective as to a planet itself. If you have a computer program that lists midpoints, print out a list of them by sign and see what you have. If you have ever wondered why a particular spot on your chart seems to be sensitive to transits, despite the fact that there are no planets there, a bunch of midpoints may be the answer.

The nodes of the Moon

The path that the Sun and the planets appear to take around our world is called the ecliptic. The Moon's orbit around the Earth travels slightly upwards and downwards diagonally across the ecliptic. The point where the Moon crosses on its northward journey is called the north node ☊ and the point where it recrosses the ecliptic, two weeks later, in a southerly direction is called the south node ☋.

Traditional Indian astrologers call these Rahu – the dragon's head – and Kethu – the dragon's tail. Indian astrologers consider the nodes to be *karmic* points, with the south node showing the lessons learned in a previous life, and the north node showing what has to be learned in this one. I have recently discovered that some astrologers reverse this concept, considering the north node to be what one already knows! Some Western astrologers consider the north node to be those areas where a subject finds it easy to fit in with prevailing social and political circumstances. The south node would therefore suggest areas where the subject is out of step with current political and social thinking.

In predictive astrology, I have often found the nodes connecting some of the more practical aspects of lunar activity. Therefore something like a move of house or a major domestic upheaval may be shown by a progression or transit to the nodes. The same goes for dealings with family members, especially the older female relatives. This is not to say that the karmic or 'political correctness' of the nodes doesn't count; it is just a case of examining the subject's situation and seeing what fits. In some cases, karmic relationships seem to show up on the nodes. In other cases, matters relating to unfinished business seem to be attracted by these strange points. I shall give you some idea of how to cope with these in the interpretation section later in this book.

Planetoids, asteroids and moons

Some years ago, when I first heard Chiron mentioned, it was referred to as an asteroid, but nowadays astrologers are calling it a planetoid. Chiron is not a moon or satellite of any planet, but a large lump of rock that is orbiting the Sun in its own right, as do the thousands of asteroids. You may have heard the old saying that 'size doesn't matter'. Well, in the solar system this may well be the case! Pluto, which is a small planet, has its own satellite called Charon (pronounced Karon or Sharon), which is a third its size. Our own satellite, the Moon, is quite large, being the size of Asia! Mars has two moons called Phobos and Demos, while Jupiter, Saturn, Neptune and Uranus have many moons, with new ones being discovered all the time. However, tiny Chiron appears to be important, so I shall include it in the interpretation section of this book.

There are many asteroids, and here are the names of some of them: Ceres, Pallas Athene, Juno, Vesta, Psyche, Eros, Lilith, Toro, Sappho, Amor, Pandora, Icarus, Diana, Hidalgo, Urania.

Arabic parts

Over the ages, astrologers from various cultures have invented a variety of systems, and the Arabs used one that they called 'parts'. Although these were used principally in natal charting to show the areas of life where a subject would succeed and be happy or where they would experience difficulties, these 'parts' were also employed predictively, by watching the planets cross them or make other aspects to them.

The one part that has lingered on in modern astrology is the *part of fortune*. This is found by adding the longitude of the Moon to that of the ascendant and then subtracting the longitude of the Sun. However, when a subject is born at night, the process must be reversed, thus *adding* the longitude of the Sun and *subtracting* that of the Moon. Confused? Well, don't be, because it isn't as complicated as it looks. If you are at all used to geometry or to using a compass, this will come easily; if not, just take a little longer to think about what you're doing. The chances are that you will find the part of fortune on any computer program, but whether this is calculated for births after dark as well as during the day is not always obvious.

Example

Now let us take our calculators and look at an example. Jane was born during the day. Her ascendant is 14 degrees of Taurus, her Moon is 20 degrees of Scorpio and her Sun is 7 degrees of Leo.

Ascendant, 14 Taurus, + Moon, 20 degrees Scorpio	= 216 degrees
Ascendant, 14 Taurus, – Sun, 7 degrees Leo	= 83 degrees
	133 degrees

Ascendant, 14 Taurus, + 133 degrees = 27 degrees Virgo.

Therefore Jane's part of fortune is 27 degrees Virgo.

If we use an equal house chart, this part would be in Jane's fifth house. Therefore Jane is most likely to make her fortune by working hard at creative ventures, or she may succeed by working with children. Maybe she could make a success of running a glamorous health and diet club for stressed-out lady executives! Furthermore, any transit or progression to Jane's part of fortune would bring opportunities or difficulties in achieving her goals in life.

There are many of these 'parts' and not all of them have to be reversed for after-dark births. Here are just a few of the formulae for those of you who may fancy having a go at some of them for yourselves.

Part	*Formula*	*Reverse at night*
Fortune	Asc. + Moon – Sun	Yes
Spirit	Asc. + Sun – Moon	Yes
Friendship/love	Asc. + Spirit – Fortune	Yes
Trickery/deception	Asc. + Venus – Sun	No
Marriage (men)	Asc. + Venus – Saturn	No
Marriage (women)	Asc. + Saturn – Venus	No

If you want to delve more deeply into this area of astrology, you will need a book called *The Fortunes of Astrology* by Robert Hurtz Granite, which is listed in the further reading section.

The fixed stars

To modern people like us, the term 'fixed stars' simply means *stars*, and covers all the stars that can be seen with the naked eye – with the exception of our own Sun. The reason that the ancient astronomer/astrologers called the stars *fixed* is simply that they didn't appear to move around the Earth in the way that the Sun, Moon and planets did. Nowadays we know that our own Sun is a small star, close to the outer edge of a huge galaxy. We also know that the whole galaxy is on the move.

A list of the fixed stars can be found in issue number four of a wonderful magazine called *The Traditional Astrologer*. This list gives an idea of how the stars work on a chart by associating them with one or two planets that operate in similar ways. For example, I have the fixed star of the first (alpha) magnitude,

Aldebaran, on my Uranus in Gemini. This adds a Mars-like attitude to my Uranus in the twelfth house. Does this make me a very perceptive and aggressive astrologer? How would one of your own fixed stars react to a transit or a progression to another planet? Get the list and try it out for yourself.

15

How to Find Your Way through the Interpretation Maze

THE BEST WAY to interpret a chart is to do it *logically*. Find a routine that suits you and stick to it and, unless you are already an accomplished astrologer, keep things very simple. Use only the normal and very obvious planets and features on a chart and deal with only the major aspects. In time you will find a system that suits you, but, in case you really don't know where to start, I shall show you mine. At the end of this chapter you will find a very abbreviated interpretation of a progressed chart. The reason that I have kept this interpretation so very brief is that the most interesting form of astrology is the kind you do for yourself, with the charts of people or things that are dear to your own heart.

Stage 1

First of all make up a natal chart and then work out a set of day-for-a-year progressions. Place the progressions around the natal chart (using a different coloured ink, if working by hand) and also make a separate list of them to refer to. Keep a notebook handy for your findings. Check the interpretations section of this book for a quick insight into their meanings, and treat yourself in due course to some of the other books that are listed in the further reading section.

Look through everything in the following order.

A *method for using day-for-a-year progressions*

1. The midheaven: Check for changes of sign or house and any major aspect to any planet or angle. This could be a conjunction, opposition, square, sextile or trine (also include the inconjunct). Jot down your findings in your notebook. Anything that affects the midheaven is always important. After checking to see if this makes any aspects to anything on the natal chart, look to see if it makes any aspects to anything that is progressed.
2. The ascendant: Check for everything in the same way as per the midheaven. This will probably not be as influential in its effects as the midheaven.
3. Pluto: This won't move enough by progression during a lifetime to be worth considering.
4. Neptune: This won't move enough by progression during a lifetime to be worth considering.
5. Uranus: Unless your subject is very old indeed, this won't have travelled far enough to be worth considering.
6. Saturn: If your subject is elderly this will be worth a glance, but it moves very slowly.
7. Jupiter: This is definitely worth looking at. Check for sign and house changes, aspects and retrograde motion. Also look for aspects to other progressions.
8. Mars: Check as per Jupiter.
9. Venus: Check as per Jupiter.
10. Mercury: Check as per Jupiter.
11. The Sun: Check as per Jupiter. Remember that the Sun never goes retrograde.
12. Chiron: If you decide to use Chiron, check as per Jupiter.
13. The nodes of the Moon: If you decide to use these, you may find that they haven't moved enough to make any fresh aspects.
14. The part of fortune: This is unlikely to be worth using at all, but if you have it on your computer just glance at the sign and house it now occupies.
15. The Moon: This is the most important part of the whole reading, and it will probably take you as long to work

through this section as it has all the others put together. Take your time over this. Firstly, check to see what sign and house the Moon has progressed into. Bear in mind that the Moon moves at roughly a degree for a year, so it is easy to work out how long it has been in its current sign and house, and how much longer it will be before it changes. Look this up in the relevant chapter and also in the progressed Moon section of my book *Moon Signs*. Check out the meaning of the Moon through the signs and houses in any other predictive books you can get your hands on as well.

Now check the actual degree of the progressed Moon and work it forward until it makes an aspect to another planet or to some other feature on the natal chart. Bearing in mind that the Moon moves one degree per month, make a note of the date of any event. Now continue to move the Moon forward and check each event in turn. You may find that several months go by with nothing much happening, followed by a period when a whole bunch of aspects occur at once or hard upon each other's heels. Note down the dates of everything and also the interpretations. If you want to check that this works, try moving the Moon *backwards* and see how it connected to other planets and features and examine what happened at those times.

Stage 2

If you have coped happily with the day-for-a-year progressions, find your ephemeris and look at the transits against everything on the natal and the progressed chart. Whether you choose to use your transits against the natal chart alone or against both the natal and the progressed positions, the following list should help you to work out a logical order in which to proceed.

A method for using transits

1. Pluto: Check for the sign and house this is in and any aspects that it makes to any planet or angle. Pluto's orbit is eccentric but very slow, so it will affect any sensitive spot

on a chart for a year or two, or even more if Pluto is retrograde over a particular spot. Pluto spends many years in each sign.

2. Neptune: As per Pluto. Neptune's effect can be felt for well over a year, possibly even a couple of years. Neptune spends 11 to 12 years in each sign.
3. Uranus: As per Pluto. Uranus's effect can be felt for a year or more. Uranus spends around seven years in each sign.
4. Saturn: As per Pluto. Saturn's effect can be felt for several months, sometimes even up to a year. Saturn spends two to two and a half years in each sign.
5. Jupiter: As per Pluto. Jupiter's effect can be felt for a few months. It spends just over a year in each sign.
6. Mars: As per Pluto. Mars's effect usually lasts only for a matter of weeks, but if it spends some time in retrograde motion its consequences can be felt for several months.
7. Venus: As per Pluto. Venus transits last for up to a month, but take note of those times when Venus is retrograde, because this can lengthen and intensify its effects.
8. Mercury: As per Pluto. Mercury's transits last for a couple of weeks; however, watch out for retrograde times.
9. Chiron: This planetoid has an eccentric orbit, but it usually spends a couple of years in a sign. Its transits can therefore last for several months, especially when it turns retrograde and back again.
10. The nodes of the Moon: These take about a year or so to work through each sign, and their effect can last for a few months when aspecting a particularly sensitive spot.
11. The Moon: The Moon takes two and a half days to work through each sign, so its transits are very short lived. However a new Moon, a full Moon and especially an eclipse will have a powerful effect on anything that it aspects. An eclipse which conjuncts a subject's Sun, Moon or ascendant is bound to be strongly felt.

You will soon notice, if you haven't already, that the outer planets are virtually useless for this kind of progression, while the inner planets are not much use for transits. This is why a combination of progressions and transits is so good: it covers just about everything.

When looking at other methods such as solar arcs and solar returns, look at all you can! I have suggested an order of work later in this chapter.

A cautionary tale

When I was in the early stages of working as a professional consultant, I read anything and everything I could get my hands on. Many of the books were written in the pompous, pseudo-psychological style that was in vogue in the 1970s. All these wonderful (usually American) astrologers went to great pains to explain that they prepared a pile of charts and worked hard on them, well in advance of their clients actually coming for their appointments. All I can say is that these great astrologers couldn't have come across some of the idiots with whom I have had to deal.

Time after time, I would prepare my charts (by hand in those days, of course), only to be told when the client turned up that they had given me the wrong details. My client would cheerfully announce, 'I phoned my Mum and she told me that I wasn't born at three in the afternoon but at two thirty in the morning', or 'I thought I was born in Birmingham but it was my sister who was born there, I was actually born in Bristol.' Many people didn't know the difference between am and pm, and admitted that they had given me the wrong meridian! This was often accompanied by the ingenuous comment, 'does it matter?' Needless to say, I soon learned to put a hand-drawn chart together with the client actually sitting there alongside me. Oddly enough, the clients enjoyed watching me draw up 'their' details, and the time spent quietly sitting and watching this process helped them to relax and to forget the cares of the world they had left behind outside my workroom. It is probable that looking at their charts opened a chakra or two in the same way that occurs when looking at tarot cards being laid out, and that helped me to reach into them psychically as well as astrologically!

A far more frustrating and all too common situation was to actually do the job and see the client happily off the premises, only to have them ring back the next day. The tentative voice on the phone saying that mum has now told him/her that the birth time (or date or place – or all three) was wrong! They took it very badly when I told them that, if they wanted the job done again, they would have to pay for it again. They couldn't see why two or three hours of my time shouldn't be thrown away. Astrologers are usually kindly souls who want to go out and help people, but there are times when we could happily strangle them!

Oddly enough, if the birth time as given *is* wrong, this isn't quite the disaster in progressed work that it is in natal charting. This is because, most of the time, you are looking at planetary movements rather than worrying too much about the nature of the person. Events will be fairly easy to spot even with a mistaken birth time. The same goes for cases where the birth time is not known at all, because it is still possible to get some useful information from a 'flat' or 'natural' chart where your ascendant or starting-point is always nought degrees of Aries. In these cases, you won't have the houses to play with, and the Moon position could be out by a few degrees, but it is surprising how much information you can glean out of even this kind of half-hearted job. You may even find yourself gradually rectifying the chart and actually finding the ascendant as you go along. The moral of all this is not to become upset when things are not perfect, and to be prepared to 'jiggle' a suspect chart in order to get things right. Time and practice will give you a feel for this kind of work. It may also make you realize how much nicer it would be to work as a crossing-sweeper!

Other types of progressed chart

If you are dealing with a solar arc type of chart where all the planets and other features have been moved forward by one degree, simply find an order that seems logical and proceed with it. If you need a suitable method, try each of the following progressed planets and see if they have changed sign or house or if they are aspecting anything else on the chart.

Solar and lunar returns can be dealt with in the same order or in any other order that you feel is logical. Remember that different methods of progression place differing emphasis on the planets, angles, etc. For instance, the day-for-a-year method places an extremely strong emphasis on the progressed Moon. The sign and house through which this is travelling is vitally important, and a lunar aspect is often the trigger for any number of important events. When dealing with the returns, the midheaven and ascendant move up the scale of importance. In solar arc progressions everything seems to be of equal weight, with the Sun being just that little bit out in front.

The progressed planet or angle
The Sun
The Moon
Mercury
Venus
Mars
Jupiter
Saturn
Uranus
Neptune
Pluto
The ascendant (also the descendant)
The midheaven (also the nadir)
The nodes (if you wish)
Chiron (if you wish)
The part of fortune (if you wish)

16

Astrology and the Human Body

CHECK OUT the following list to see how the planets, signs and houses link to the different parts of the body. This list will come in very handy when you want to examine the state of health of a subject on a progressed chart of any kind. The information here will be far too basic for those who want to make a career of medical astrology but it is enough for the rest of us. Think before opening your mouth when dealing with this aspect of astrology because the last thing you want to do is to alarm anyone or to plant the idea in a subject's head that he is likely to become ill.

Aries, first house, Mars

Part of body

The head, brain, eyes, skull and upper jaw; also the pineal gland and arteries to the head and brain.

Potential ailments

Headaches, acne, fainting, neuralgia, fevers of the brain.

Taurus, second house, Venus

Part of body

The lower jaw, the throat – including the thyroid gland – the neck, larynx, chin, ears, tongue, vocal chords, the upper (cervical) spine, the jugular vein, the tonsils.

Potential ailments
Laryngitis, throat inflammation, over/underactive thyroid, goitre, tonsillitis.

Gemini, third house, Mercury

Part of body
The upper respiratory system, the shoulders, arms, wrists, hands and fingers, and the upper ribs.

Potential ailments
Bronchitis, asthma, chest disorders, accidents to arms, shoulders and hands. Also diseases of the nervous system and the mind.

Cancer, fourth house, the Moon

Part of body
The lungs, breasts, rib cage, stomach and digestive organs, alimentary canal, sternum, womb and pancreas.

Potential ailments
Gastric disorders, heartburn, obesity.

Leo, fifth house, the Sun

Part of body
The spine – especially the upper back – the spinal cord, the heart, the arteries – especially the aorta – the circulation, the spleen.

Potential ailments
Back complaints, spinal meningitis, heart diseases.

Virgo, sixth house, Mercury (and Chiron?)

Part of body
The lower digestive system, the bowels, the lower dorsal nerves, the skin, the nervous system and the mind.

Potential ailments

Bowel diseases, indigestion, colic, intestinal infection. Also skin infections and nervous or stress-related disorders. Let us not forget hypochondria!

Libra, seventh house, Venus

Part of body

The bladder, kidneys, lumbar region, haunches to buttocks, adrenal glands, lumbar nerves and blood vessels.

Potential ailments

Kidney and bladder disorders, eczema, lumbago, abscesses.

Scorpio, eighth house, Pluto (and Mars)

Part of body

The reproductive and sexual organs – especially the cervix – the lower stomach, the lower spine including the coccyx, the groin, anus, genito-urinary system and prostate gland, and the eyes.

Potential ailments

Bladder disorders, genito-urinary diseases, prostate or menstrual problems, piles.

Sagittarius, ninth house, Jupiter

Part of body

The hips and thighs, the pelvis, the sacrum, the liver, the sciatic nerve, the arterial system – especially the femoral artery.

Potential ailments

Injuries and diseases of hips, thighs and pelvis. Sciatica, liver disorders, paralysis of limbs.

Capricorn, tenth house, Saturn

Part of body

The skin, ears, teeth, bones, knees and bones above and below the knees.

Potential ailments

Rheumatism, skin complaints, knee injuries, bone diseases. Chronic ailments of any kind.

Aquarius, eleventh house, Uranus (and Saturn)

Part of body

The ankles, calves and shins, breathing, the circulatory system – especially to the extremities.

Potential ailments

Calf and ankle injuries, varicose veins, poor circulation, blood diseases, heart palpitations.

Pisces, twelfth house, Neptune (and Jupiter)

Part of body

The feet and toes, lungs, lymphatic system and pituitary gland. Furthermore, the mind, and the 'ethereal body' – that is, the bit that can become upset by psychic disturbances or imbalances in the aura or the psychic system.

Potential ailments

Bunions, chilblains, tendonitis in the feet, drink and drug problems, lymphatic and glandular disorders. Also strange allergies, mysterious ailments, sleep disturbances. Those who have strong Moon or Neptune involvements on their charts may respond very well to alternative therapies, especially homoeopathy.

17

Decans or Decanates

EACH SIGN of the zodiac can be divided into three decans – more commonly known as decanates. Each decanate comprise ten degrees and each one is assigned to a sign within the same element as the whole sign. This is simpler when expressed as a list.

The fire group			
Aries:	0°–10°	First decanate	– Aries
	11°–20°	Second decanate	– Leo
	21°–30°	Third decanate	– Sagittarius
Leo:	0°–10°	First decanate	– Leo
	11°–20°	Second decanate	– Sagittarius
	21°–30°	Third decanate	– Aries
Sagittarius:	0°–10°	First decanate	– Sagittarius
	11°–20°	Second decanate	– Aries
	21°–30°	Third decanate	– Leo
The earth group			
Taurus:	0°–10°	First decanate	– Taurus
	11°–20°	Second decanate	– Virgo
	21°–30°	Third decanate	– Capricorn
Virgo:	0°–10°	First decanate	– Virgo
	11°–20°	Second decanate	– Capricorn
	21°–30°	Third decanate	– Taurus
Capricorn:	0°–10°	First decanate	– Capricorn
	11°–20°	Second decanate	– Taurus
	21°–30°	Third decanate	– Virgo

The air group			
Gemini:	0°–10°	First decanate	– Gemini
	11°–20°	Second decanate	– Libra
	21°–30°	Third decanate	– Aquarius
Libra:	0°–10°	First decanate	– Libra
	11°–20°	Second decanate	– Aquarius
	21°–30°	Third decanate	– Gemini
Aquarius:	0°–10°	First decanate	– Aquarius
	11°–20°	Second decanate	– Gemini
	21°–30°	Third decanate	– Libra
The water group			
Cancer:	0°–10°	First decanate	– Cancer
	11°–20°	Second decanate	– Scorpio
	21°–30°	Third decanate	– Pisces
Scorpio:	0°–10°	First decanate	– Scorpio
	11°–20°	Second decanate	– Pisces
	21°–30°	Third decanate	– Cancer
Pisces:	0°–11°	First decanate	– Pisces
	11°–20°	Second decanate	– Cancer
	21°–30°	Third decanate	– Scorpio

What do the decanates mean?

In natal astrology, the decanates modify the effect of the planets as they travel through the signs. For example, a person born with Mercury in the third decanate of Scorpio (which is sub-ruled by Cancer) would have a less incisive but more intuitive type of mind than if Mercury were in the first decanate. A person with Venus in the third decanate of Virgo (sub-ruled by Taurus) would be far more sensual than the average Venus in Virgo subject. In predictive astrology, a planet moving through a sign will also be modified by the decanate of the sign it passes through.

Thus, if you discovered that your Mars was now moving into the last – Aries – decanate of Leo, you could expect to be more assertive than ever before. Alternatively, if your Jupiter was entering the second – Cancer – decanate of Pisces, you could expect to become more attuned to the financial and other benefits of a home and family than the journey through Pisces might otherwise suggest.

Part Three

A Guide to Interpretation

Introducing Part Three

There are a number of large astrology books on the market that offer in-depth interpretations of the planetary movements. Some of these cover transits while others are concerned with progressions. You can use the same interpretations for either transits or progressions because the information is the same for both. For example, a transit or a progression of Venus to your natal Sun is a pleasant thing to experience. The difference being that a transit will be around for a few days, while a progression brings a couple of years or more of Venusian growth.

There isn't enough room in this book to go into everything in depth, so I have barely touched upon the psychological and spiritual implications of these planetary movements. However, even a brief and rather bald interpretation is better than nothing and it will help to get you off the ground. As it happens, you may find you prefer this practical approach.

I had to make choices about how best to present this information, so I have shown how the planets work when moving through the various signs and houses and when in easy or difficult aspects. For instance, you will find *happy* aspects such as the sextile and the trine lumped together. This is all well and good, but it may be worth bearing in mind that these two aspects do work slightly differently, with the sextile doing its good work on a mental or logical level and the trine on a more emotional or feeling level. All this is explained in greater detail as you move through the chapters. I have taken the Moon onto a deeper level, because it is probably the most important factor that you are going to be faced with when dealing with day-for-a-year progressions.

I have also provided summaries of the solar and lunar movements and this should be a great help to those of you who are beginners to this kind of astrology.

18

The Sun through the Signs and Houses

Timescale

BY DAY-FOR-A-YEAR progression, the Sun will spend 30 years traversing a sign. If you use the equal house method, it will take the same time to cross a house. But it will take only a month to cross a sign or a 30 degree equal house by transit. The Sun never travels retrograde.

Correspondences

The fifth house and Leo.

The body

The Sun rules the spine – especially the upper back – the spinal cord, the heart and arteries – especially the aorta – the circulation and the spleen. However, do refer back to Chapter 16 to see which areas of the body might be affected by the progression of the Sun through the signs and houses.

Character

Solar progressions and transits always indicate important experiences. In theory, this should affect the public aspects of your life rather than personal feelings or domestic and family matters. Beneficial aspects can bring success in any area of life, happiness in connection with children, holidays, amusements and a fun-filled love life. Adverse aspects can bring great suffering and hardship, but these can be character building and much can be learned from them. Spiritual lessons may have to be learned at such times.

The elements

You need to bear in mind that the Sun is a ball of fire, and it is associated with the fire sign of Leo. This means that the Sun is at its most comfortable and effective when traversing any of the fire signs, whether this be by transit or progression. The Sun is fairly compatible with air signs, less so with earth signs and at its least comfortable when journeying through water signs.

The Sun through Aries or the first house

If your Sun moves away from Pisces or the twelfth house, you will face the fact that you have reached the end of a phase and are now ready to start something new. New ideas, aims, ambitions, renewed energy and a 'kick-start' can be applied to your life. There will be satisfaction from looking back to what has been done in the past, but also impatience to get on with the new phase. You will gradually notice yourself becoming more outgoing and Arian in nature. You could start to take an interest in Arian jobs, such as teaching, social work, the armed forces or other large organizations, and you may take up hobbies such as engineering or car maintenance.

Beneficial aspects to the Sun at this time will open the doors of opportunity. This would be a good time to seek favours, promotion or advancement and to deal with superiors. Challenging aspects could bring illness, a lack of energy, trouble at work and a loss of position or prestige. Difficult aspects can also bring great benefits, but these will be hard won.

Summary

- More outgoing and egotistic behaviour
- New interests
- Seeking personal advancement in politics or career

The Sun through Taurus or the second house

Movement into this sign or house exerts a calming influence and makes you less impulsive, less apt to take up sudden enthusiasms, while growing more reliable and sensible instead. If you have been a bit footloose up to now, you will soon settle into a job and family life, and make as much of a go of it as possible. You will be more stubborn and you may develop a stick-in-the-mud attitude, but you will also be more inclined to put down roots. Your life will be less eventful, but anything that does occur will be more profound than before. Your attitude will be friendly and sociable and you may take up creative Taurean hobbies such as gardening, the fashion trade, building and cooking. You will need to guard against developing a sweet tooth and giving yourself a weight problem. You make an effort to obtain and to keep money and possessions. You will search for and find your own value system, if necessary, rejecting that of your parents and school teachers.

Beneficial aspects to the Sun in this sign or house bring money, property and goods, as well as beauty, harmony and comfort. Challenging ones can temporarily remove these things or make them harder to obtain.

Summary

- Stubborn and determined attitude
- Desire to have and to hold
- Behaviour is more cooperative and sociable
- Need for beauty, harmony
- Love of pretty things
- Examination of personal value system

The Sun through Gemini or the third house

When the Sun moves into this sign or house, you will want to give up some of your more materialistic ways in favour of a more intellectual approach. You will be happy to study and to pass on information to others and you will become more perceptive and critical. Life will hold more variety and you will be more versatile and dexterous, brighter but also more restless. Local travel will become more important and there will be much contact with neighbours, siblings and colleagues.

When the Sun is well aspected, negotiations, intellectual pursuits and contacts with others will progress well. Under challenging aspects these things will prove to be a struggle, but intellectual and other benefits can accrue as a result of efforts being made.

Summary

- Seeking intellectual challenges
- Seeking variety
- More ambitious
- Learning to negotiate

The Sun through Cancer or the fourth house

When the Sun progresses into this sign or house, you will want to be less of a rolling stone and more of a stable family person. You could set up a home, open a small business or become more involved with the members of your family under this influence. You may feel more attached to your mother and to other older women. History and the past will begin to fascinate you and you could start to collect things that have some special meaning for you. This isn't a particularly comfortable placement for the Sun, because your feelings are made more sensitive and painful.

Easy aspects will bring luck with property, family matters and any work that is carried out in the home. Difficult aspects could disrupt these elements of life or make it hard to achieve a happy family life. The feelings could be very tender when tough aspects occur.

Summary

- Desire for home or premises
- Family life becomes important
- Contact with women
- Could become a collector
- Feelings more sensitive

The Sun through Leo or the fifth house

This being the Sun's natural sign or house, it is at its best here. You should become more 'centred' or, in plain English, happier about yourself and about your way of life. You will be more egotistic or arrogant, but also more successful in everything you do, so you will probably deserve the right to become somewhat insufferable! You will develop into a more powerful figure and you will be happy to display any extra wealth, extra possessions, talents or anything else that you gain under this influence. You may become concerned with those things that are attached to this sign or house, such as creative work, show business, dealing with children and young people or working in the leisure industry. Your attitude to business will be less cautious and more flamboyant and entrepreneurial.

Under beneficial aspects, you can reach for the stars and get just about anything that you want from life, but under difficult ones you could lose most of your gains – for a while at least. However, you won't stay down for long and your optimistic mood will soon return.

Summary

- Desire for leisure activities
- Travel for fun
- Attachment to children
- Creative ventures sought
- Interest in glamour
- Need to be the centre of attention
- Bossy attitude; may be overbearing

The Sun through Virgo or the sixth house

When the Sun reaches this sign or house, you become more diligent and more concerned with the needs of others. You will quieten down and get your head down in order to concentrate on specifics. Detailed work such as computing, dress-making and astrology might appeal. You will be less arrogant and more modest, less confident and outgoing and more cautious. In some ways, life becomes harder. You may become interested in sixth house matters, such as health and healing. You may also feel the urge to take up issues that are attached to the terms and conditions of other people's employment. You may take on voluntary work in a hospital or a trades union. Try to keep your confidence level high by avoiding negative or critical people and aim to avoid criticizing yourself too much. Another problem area is the Virgo habit of destroying anything that looks as if it is likely to be successful before it really materializes.

Under beneficial aspects you will turn into a good employer or employee and you will also make – and learn how to keep – money. Under challenging aspects, health or business setbacks can occur.

Summary

- More modest attitude
- Attention to details
- Interest in health and healing
- Employment of or by others becoming important
- Intellectual interests

The Sun through Libra or the seventh house

This is the beginning of a cycle that connects you to other people and makes you less self-centred or self-reliant. Marriage, partnerships and working relationships become important now, and matters such as finding a partner, splitting up from someone and changes within working partnerships can occur. If you have any enemies, they will come out into the open. You will look at value systems that are different from those with which you grew up and you will strive to put your life into balance again, if this is necessary. Libran jobs and interests may attract you, possibly leading you to take up a career as an agent or a go-between of some kind. Issues of justice and fair play also begin to play a role, and you will want to fight for what you think is right. You may become involved in legal dealings, either in connection with work or as a result of changes in your personal life. You will become more laid back, lazier and less interested in harsh reality.

Under beneficial aspects, marriage, partnerships and work

arrangements all do well, while under challenging aspects these spheres of life can become difficult. You may have to fight off enemies.

Summary

- Interest in justice and fair play
- Desire for partnerships
- Desire for harmony and balance
- Open warfare at home or out in the world
- Liaising with or between others

The Sun through Scorpio or the eighth house

This planetary movement will make you stronger and more positive about everything that you do and you may even be quite earnest and humourless at times. You will be less inclined to sit back and let things happen or to rely upon others. Psychic or spiritual matters could begin to attract you and issues of life and death will both fascinate you. You may be personally affected by life and death situations. Guard against becoming despotic or overambitious or disinclined to take the feelings of others into account. You may take up a job that involves probing or investigating. Possibilities might be surgery, oil exploration, insurance fraud investigation, forensic work, mining and so on. You will deal with legacies, mortgages, divorce settlements, shares and anything else that connects money to yourself and others. Sex and sexual relationships will become a strong force in your life now and this itself could lead to a firm commitment to a new way of life. The key idea here is of merging yourself or your money with others.

Under beneficial aspects you will gain from some of the above-mentioned ideas and you will receive karmic benefits. Under challenging aspects problems arise, and there may be karmic debts to be repaid.

Summary

- Attitude becoming more earnest
- Feelings becoming deeper

- Partnerships make or break
- Interest in the occult
- Interest in investigation of various kinds
- Karmic benefits and debts

The Sun through Sagittarius or the ninth house

The ninth house and Sagittarius are considered to be 'lucky', and the Sun is, of course, comfortable in a fire sign. You will feel the urge to expand your mental, physical and philosophical horizons in a number of ways. There will be a strong desire to break away and to increase your personal freedom. You may travel to distant places, and contacts with people from other lands and backgrounds will become important. You may work in an import/export business and it is even possible that you decide to take up with or marry a foreigner. Religion, philosophy and the spiritual side of life will start to interest you and you may discover that you have hidden talents as a medium, a healer or even an astrologer. Some people learn a lot about the law under this influence, either through their work or through personal circumstances. Teaching and learning begin to interest you. The most important issue is that you will be forced to examine your beliefs in the hunt for a philosophy of life that works for you. This may lead you to reject previous ideas and turn away from your background.

Under beneficial aspects all the ideas mentioned above will prosper, while under difficult ones you will find your beliefs challenged and your attempts to expand your mental, physical and spiritual horizons being stifled. There could be legal problems too.

Summary

- Search for personal philosophy
- Interest in spiritual matters
- Travel, foreigners, foreign goods become important
- Desire for freedom
- Legal matters could occur
- Education and training
- Karmic benefits

The Sun through Capricorn or the tenth house

You will begin to reach for the top now, becoming more ambitious and serious in your attitudes. This sign and house are very much associated with banking, finance and big business, and therefore these will become an important part of your life. You will seek financial security, roots and status and this will lead to a more materialistic attitude. Politics, publicity and prominence would all become important now. You could grow more attached to your parents, especially a father or father figure, at this time and you will have more sympathy with older people in general.

Under beneficial aspects you reach the top of the heap, but under difficult ones you would fall from grace. Guard against becoming coldly ambitious at the expense of fun or of your personal relationships.

Summary

- Ambition and goal orientation
- Interest in parents or older people
- Desire for financial stability
- Desire for status

The Sun through Aquarius or the eleventh house

When the Sun moves into this sign or house you won't be any less ambitious, but your goals will be different. Your outlook will be less self-centred and more universal. You will take an interest in humanitarian or environmental issues or any number of other causes. Groups that are filled with like-minded people will appeal and you may become involved with unions, or local or national governments. You will be interested in studying and also teaching, while for some of you social work will appeal. Astrology and other philosophical systems will interest you and you will become less conventional and more eccentric as time progresses. Guard against obstinacy and too independent an attitude and utilize the other Aquarian traits, such as friendliness and helpfulness. Don't allow idealism to make you lose touch with reality.

Under favourable aspects you will be happy, outgoing and fulfilled, while under challenging ones you could feel isolated and up against it.

Summary

- Group activities appeal
- Idealism and humanitarianism
- More logical, less emotional
- Eccentric
- Interest in astrology, etc.
- Teaching and learning

The Sun through Pisces or the twelfth house

You become far kinder and more spiritual under this sign. You probably won't give up worldly ambitions and become a hermit overnight, but there is bound to be a more introspective attitude. You will be more sensitive to others and much more interested in psychic or spiritual matters. Circumstances may push you into giving up some aspect of your life and to become more self-sacrificial in some way. You may choose or you may be forced to live part of your life in seclusion for a while. This may be the result of karmic debts that need to be repaid. On a practical level, you will enjoy working on creative or artistic projects and you may learn to play a musical instrument. You could also travel in connection with your work.

Under favourable aspects, artistic, creative, musical, poetic or spiritual matters will prosper. Mysterious events could occur that bring help and guidance from strange sources. Under distressing aspects, you will be lonely.

Summary

- Feelings become more sensitive
- Emotions strengthen
- Kinder attitude
- Interest in mysticism, astrology, etc.

- Karmic benefits and debts
- Self-sacrifice
- Seclusion and withdrawal

19

Interpreting the Aspects

THIS IS a quick guide to interpreting the aspects that you should find helpful. Remember when looking at progressed or transiting aspects to bear in mind the signs and, more importantly, the houses that are involved, because these will alter the way these aspects work.

Checklist

Conjunction
This has some connection to first house issues. Conjunctions can be wonderful or terrible, but even bad events will work in your interest in the long run.

Semi-sextile
This has some connection to second house issues. It has a very minor effect and could be slightly beneficial or slightly irritating. The semi-sextile may highlight concepts that you value, such as time, freedom, or material or spiritual benefits.

Sextile
This has some connection to third house issues. It is good for business, communications, people, local affairs, local travel and also matters relating to brothers, sisters and neighbours.

Square
This has some connection to fourth and tenth house issues.

The square is likely to be a difficult aspect, as the planets, signs and houses involved are uncomfortable and, possibly, incompatible with each other. This brings tension, pressure, restrictions, troubles. Authority figures may be difficult at this time.

Trine

This has some connection to fifth house issues. The trine is a creative, fun-filled, youthful, happy and relaxed aspect.

Opposition

This has some connection to seventh and some eighth house issues. It suggests that dealing with other people can bring benefits at this time, especially if you are lonely and isolated. This can be difficult if other people insist on being awkward over important matters. Joint ventures, sex and major changes can bring problems.

Inconjunct

This has some connection to sixth and eighth house issues. While this is really a minor aspect, I feel it to be too important to be dismissed lightly. This can be irritating, bringing health or work difficulties among other things. Alternatively, joint arrangements or official matters may be trying.

The remaining minor aspects are harder to pin down by this method.

Putting it all together

A little intuition, in addition to the ability to hold all the relevant factors in your mind, is the way to make this form of astrology work. Although this sounds difficult, it isn't. All those people whom I have taught over the years have found that it comes easily and naturally. Try running through the following list as you work on your chart until you get the hang of things.

Checklist

1. The planets, angles or other features that are involved in an aspect
2. The nature of the aspect that is being made
3. The signs that are involved
4. The houses that are involved
5. Complex aspects, i.e., those that involve more than two planets or other features

20

Solar Conjunctions

Sun conjunct Sun

THIS IS KNOWN to astrologers as the solar return and to everyone else as a birthday! Have a happy one! This should be a time of celebration, renewal and increased confidence, but for various reasons it is often a time of regret and fear of getting old. What a shame!

Sun conjunct Moon

Anything to do with the home and family will go well. Dealing with women, pregnancy and other female matters are well starred. Business relating to property or the family is favoured. It is a good time to celebrate with the family.

Sun conjunct Mercury

New ideas will be buzzing around your head. You will stretch yourself mentally by learning something new, by teaching or by taking an interest in intellectual games. You could even decide to write a book! Contacts with others increase and there could be the start of a working or a personal partnership. If you need to impress the boss, or even to become the boss, this is a good time to do so. Young people will play a large part in your life and there may be more than the usual amount of contact with brothers and sisters. Work matters will go well and health will improve. You may begin working in the health or alternative therapy field. Guard against overconfidence and speaking out of turn.

Sun conjunct Venus

This will bring a happy time with plenty to celebrate and to enjoy. Your income should increase and you should feel that everything you do has a point to it. You may live a more comfortable and luxurious life, and partnerships will bring money into your life rather than suck funds out of it. Children will make you happy, you will look and feel better and a successful romance is possible. Guard against laziness, self-indulgence, and too much desire for something or somebody. Even enemies will be more open in their approach to you!

Sun conjunct Mars

This is a powerful aspect that should be great if you remember not to overdo things. You will become more self-assertive, more active and energetic, and your sex-life should receive a tremendous boost! You will become more competitive and ambitious now both for yourself and on behalf of any children with whom you are involved. You may take an interest in sporting activities. Guard against rashness, silly accidents, danger from fire or sharp instruments, and losing your friends by becoming aggressive towards them.

Sun conjunct Jupiter

This brings happiness and good fortune for you and for those who are around you, but it can also land you with some quite devastating losses. Astrologers tend to forget that Jupiter is a hot-tempered god who throws down thunderbolts on those who get on his nerves! This can mark a period of confusion, because pain and loss will be accompanied by terrific opportunities for advancement, thus bringing both positive and negative stresses at the same time. A great deal of faith in oneself and in one's capacity to cope with life will be needed at this time. However, on the whole this can be seen as a positive aspect, with doors opening in business matters and some wonderful chances for improving your financial position. Women with this transit could meet the man of their dreams or give birth to a much wanted child. Both sexes will meet new people who will be useful both as business contacts and as friends. You may take up an interest in educational, legal or spiritual matters at this time. Travel for business or for fun is well starred. A foreigner could enter your life now.

Sun conjunct Saturn

Although a conjunction is a very beneficial aspect, Saturn can cast a cloud over the Sun, making life quite hard for a while. Any effort will be rewarded, though, and the ultimate outcome of any problem will be favourable. This is a great time to make strides in a career, to look for political or social advancement and to raise your status at home and at work. Help will come from those who are in positions of authority or responsibility, and you will reach such a position yourself by the time this transit is over. Too many responsibilities will weigh heavily on your shoulders and you may have to become older than your years overnight. Your strength and endurance will be tested and you will have to develop patience and the ability to concentrate on detailed work. Your confidence may temporarily desert you. However, honour, money and a greater sense of self-worth will be the *eventual* outcome. Bear in mind the house and sign in which this occurs because this will show where the pressures are likely to be heaviest and the rewards greatest.

Sun conjunct Uranus

Something dramatic is bound to happen under this aspect and it could take almost any form. Contact with new concepts, particularly those of a scientific nature, are possible, as are strange romantic affairs or a sudden break with the past in some way. Friends may become closely associated with your life and you may decide that their company is much more important to you than your own family's. You could identify with a particular group of people who may or may not have some really strange ideas. You will turn against greed, materialism and the need for security, searching instead for new experiences and adventures in life. Your level of consciousness will be raised and you may want to take up an interest in something completely different. Astrology would be a good choice!

On 28 September 1977, Uranus made an exact transit to my husband's natal Sun/Mercury conjunction in the fifth house in Scorpio. I had been dreading the outcome of this for years and keeping my fears to myself. To be honest, I wondered whether he would die as a result of an electric shock. Well, in a way, he did just that! Just under a year before we discovered that he had a serious heart condition, and on the appointed date he had a quadruple coronary bypass. This operation was in its infancy in those days, and it required the 'switching off' of his heart by a DC current being passed through it. For the next five hours his heart and lungs were powered by a machine, and after the operation he was 'switched on' again by an AC current to the heart! Remember that the Sun is associated with the heart – as is the fifth house. Mercury suggests the use of the surgeon's skilled hands and instruments, Uranus would suggest new concepts and clever machinery. Of course, there is no sign like Scorpio for beating the grim reaper! This shows that such an awful transit *can* be survived. Incidentally, Tony is in fine fettle now, with no more heart trouble from that day to this. This incident changed his view of life completely, because up to that date he had always been ultra-cautious about taking chances on life. He was particularly circumspect about spending money. He lost his materialistic approach that day and gained a sense of adventure instead.

Sun conjunct Neptune

There is a line from a song in the musical film *Pal Joey* which goes, 'Dreams and drive are oft related, Sigmund Freud has always stated.' So when under the influence of Neptunian dreams, almost anything could happen.

As an astrologer, anything to do with Neptune worries me, because when this lovely orb becomes involved in a major progression or transit it can cause chaos. The trouble is that nothing is crystal clear when Neptune is around, and it can make you feel as though you are living in a kind of jet-lag-filled half-light. On the good side, if you have this transit to face, anything of an artistic or creative nature will be enhanced. You could take an interest in film, photography, art, music, drama, dance or anything else that lifts the spirit. You should begin to develop strong psychic abilities and you may take an interest in spiritual development or mysticism of various kinds. Telepathy, past lives, ESP, ghost hunting and precognitive dreams may become part of your life. There may be an attachment to places of seclusion, such as hospitals, prisons, etc., and you yourself could want to hide away for a while.

Needless to say, love affairs are likely to play a big part in this aspect, but they will be the romantic, secret kind with plenty of yearning, longing and waiting by the phone. If you can release your sexual and romantic tension by finding a way of expressing your feelings artistically, then you may just survive the experience. Guard against unwanted problems such as unexpected pregnancy or a too strong attachment to escapism via alcohol, overeating, gambling or drugs. If you can take up swimming, chiropody, fishing, alternative healing, novel writing, ballroom dancing or any other Neptunian pursuit, you will be using this conjunction in a positive way.

Sun conjunct Pluto

You may have to gain control of a situation and learn how to take up the reins of power. Business matters of all kinds will come to the fore now, especially those that involve joint finances. You could have to deal with taxes, mortgages, liquidation, wills, legacies and legal matters, either on your own behalf or on behalf of others. There will be enforced beginnings and endings to face and you could have to transform your life in a big way. There will surely be a number of births and deaths in your circle. You may also have to face up to some kind of sexual matter, and this could be at the heart of the beginning or the ending of a major personal relationship. Some people have deeply interesting or disturbing psychic experiences under such Pluto aspects.

Sun conjunct Chiron

Matters related to health and healing come to the fore at this time. Therefore you may struggle against health problems yourself or you may become involved with others who are sick in some way. You could become interested in work related to healing, helping, caring and teaching. You may take up an active hobby now. Another possibility is that you will either be tied to a particular situation for a while or that you may break out of a restrictive lifestyle.

Sun conjunct nodes

When the Sun crosses the north node, anything that you fancy taking up should be extremely successful. House moves and family matters will prosper. You may be able to use some kind of previous life experience in a novel way. There is a feeling that fate is with you, and anybody whom you meet at this time will prove to be good to you.

When the Sun crosses the south node the situation is not much different, but you may want to go into your shell for a little while. You could find yourself looking into history, past lives or genealogy or simply talking things over with your mother. There may be a spell of going back to old friends and lovers or picking up old skills once again for a while.

Sun conjunct ascendant

This is a time of new beginnings. Life will never be the same again. You will become more assertive and more enthusiastic about life and ready for something new. (See the Sun through the first house.)

Sun conjunct midheaven

This is a time when you will change direction and alter your goals in life. You will become more interested in worldly success and political ambitions. Your children should do well, and if you want to become a parent this would be a good time to do so. Approach people in positions of power and authority now if you need to.

Sun conjunct descendant

This is a time when relationships become more important. You may lose friends, lovers, partners, etc., from your life soon, but these will shortly be replaced by others.

Sun conjunct nadir

A time of interest in home and domestic life. You may start a family now or even found a dynasty. You could begin to look backwards rather than forwards for a while.

21

Solar Aspects

IT WOULD be nice to look at every aspect in detail and then into all the possible events that could occur under each aspect. However, in a book of this length we can take only a generalized view. Treat yourself to a few books on the interpretation of transits and use the information on these when looking at all progressions and transits. Most importantly, *offer to make up charts for your friends and predict events for them*. The feedback from this will teach you more than any other method.

Sun in happy aspect to natal Sun

This is a time of good health and self-expression. Creativity comes to the fore. Children and young people will bring joy. Romance will be fun and leisure pursuits amusing.

Sun in happy aspect to Moon

An improvement in domestic circumstances, ranging from moving house to refurbishing the one you have, is likely, as are improved family relationships and harmony between the women of the family. Children do well and there could be something to celebrate on their behalf. You will contact old friends and could even look up an ex-lover. Romance will go well, as would a holiday on or by water. Small business interests do well now, especially shops, farms and anything vaguely domestic.

Sun in happy aspect to Mercury

This is a great time to learn or teach something new. Neighbours, colleagues and friends could figure strongly in your life now, as could brothers and sisters, and all of these could come up with great ideas. A new vehicle is a possibility. You may take up an intelligent hobby or a creative venture. Negotiations will go well.

Sun in happy aspect to Venus

This brings a great improvement in your social life. Romance, friendship and everything associated with having a good time will be on the menu for you now. Art, music, dancing, leisure and pleasure will all play a part in your life at this time. You will use your charm to captivate others and your looks will improve dramatically. If you have neglected your appearance or allowed your wardrobe to go to pot, this is the time to make changes for the better.

Sun in happy aspect to Mars

These two fiery and energetic planets can combine to give you a great time. Your courage will be at its peak and you will feel that you can take on the world. This is a great time to get involved in anything especially competitive. If you decide to do something really dangerous do make sure that you take extra care, because cutting corners could cost you your life. Your raging hormones could lead you into a high-octane affair at this time! Men of influence may enter your life now and your own status and financial standing could increase. You may take up something glamorous or you may simply appear more glamorous than ever before to those who count.

Sun in happy aspect to Jupiter

This is a great time to learn something new and to explore novel ideas of all kinds. You may take a course of training at this time. If you fall in love now, it will be by finding someone who feels the same way as you do and who shares your beliefs.

You will take charge of your life and you may have considerable responsibility and leadership thrust upon you. Political aims, recognition and support are on the way to you now. You could travel or become involved with foreigners, foreign goods or foreign organizations. Legal matters would also go well.

Sun in happy aspect to Saturn

Hard work that has been done in the past will bring rewards now. Older people will be cooperative and those in positions of responsibility or authority will be approachable and helpful. You may have some extra responsibility thrust upon you but you won't be unhappy about this. Sensible people will enter your life, and any relationship that has been unsettled will steady itself down into a workable pattern. Your mood will be rather serious, and any groups or organizations that you associate with now will also have a rather serious outlook and purpose to them.

Sun in happy aspect to Uranus

You will feel an urge to break out of your usual mould and seek the freedom to be yourself and to do your own thing. You will wish to develop your creative ideas in new and original directions. Friends and like-minded groups will appeal strongly to you and these could have a marked influence on you now. You will wish to look inside yourself and to achieve your own personal goals. You may become involved with politics or causes of some kind. Novel subjects may begin to appeal to you or you could become interested in science, computers, electricity and engineering, or you may encourage children to take up these subjects. You could fall head over heels for someone to whom you feel a magnetic attraction, but it may not last.

Sun in happy aspect to Neptune

Your creative instincts will come to the fore at this time and you may wish to lend your support to people or organizations in the creative field. You could deal successfully with hospitals, institutions and homes for the elderly now. There will be an increased interest in religion, philosophy, spiritualism or even astrology, and you may seek to instruct children in these subjects. Art and music will appeal to you. You may wish to delve into your past and discover the patterns that have shaped your life. Many people experience an increase in psychic experiences at this time, especially precognitive dreams.

Sun in happy aspect to Pluto

This marks an important time of transition in your life and nothing will be the same again after this one. You may marry, divorce, take up a new career, retire, move to another country or do anything else that represents a major change of life. Guard against illness at this time and, if you do fall ill, you will need to take this into account as part of the changing pattern of your life. Business matters related to banks, tax, corporations, legacies and shared financial resources are likely to become important now. You may have to change your personal financial status as a result of the actions of others. Shared resources, such as in marriage, could become an issue. You will want to look more deeply into the meaning of everything and some aspect of investigating will become part of your life.

Sun in happy aspect to Chiron

If you or anyone in your circle has been ill lately, the situation will improve. You may become interested in alternative therapies and all other matters related to health. You could wish to help others by treating or counselling them. Teaching and learning will become important to you, especially in connection with the development of children.

Sun in happy aspect to the nodes

This would be a good time to move house or to improve the one you have. Family matters will go well and anything that you try to achieve out in the world will succeed now too. The atmosphere around you will be conducive to success and the political *Zeitgeist* will suit you. You may receive some kind of karmic benefit.

Sun in happy aspect to the ascendant

This is a good time for a fresh start and to assert yourself. New friends, increased social life and a time of fun should be around you now.

Sun in happy aspect to the midheaven

This is a great time to seek recognition, to forge ahead with career aims or simply to make up your mind as to what you want from life and then start to go out and get it. People in positions of authority should be helpful. Clean up your home, your office and your act now; you have everything to gain and nothing to lose.

Sun in challenging aspect to natal Sun

This could be a frustrating and lonely time, when others seem to be against you rather than with you. You may become intolerant or you may draw intolerance towards you. This is a bad time to ask favours, especially from those in positions of authority or responsibility, and it is unlikely that you will be able to influence anyone else either. Children could become a problem to you now, while children who undergo this aspect themselves will feel involved and misunderstood.

Sun in challenging aspect to the Moon

Family and home situations are likely to be difficult, and older women in particular could prove to be a real nuisance. You may feel at odds with yourself and it will be hard to become 'centred' at this time. Romantic situations could crumble. Arguments will arise over money and there could be some very different views of who should spend what and how in your household. Business matters may suffer, especially small businesses that you run from your own premises. Creative ventures will be difficult. The best thing is to keep to a routine, avoid arguments and try to learn as much as you can from this experience.

Sun in challenging aspect to Mercury

Try not to allow pride or intolerance to spoil things for you. Watch what you say and how you say it, because your mouth may have a tendency to run away with itself. Avoid gossip if you can. (Let's not be ridiculous; who can avoid the chance of a tasty bit of gossip?) Games and gambling are likely to go wrong and this is definitely not the time to take up competitive sports of any kind.

Sun in challenging aspect to Venus

You may become lazy under this influence, and if you're not careful you could put on a lot of weight. Exercise, the application of self-control or dedication to hard work are of no interest to you at all at this time. You may be tempted to spend money, either on your behalf or on behalf of your children, and you may not want to admit the nastier sides of their nature – or yours. Anything to do with art, beauty and creativity will be held up now and your social life will be very quiet. Family celebrations will cause hassle. Romance may go badly, but, oddly enough, your sex life could take off like a rocket.

Sun in challenging aspect to Mars

You could suddenly become quite aggressive, impulsive, argumentative and unlivable with. A competitive streak could suddenly emerge and you may become keen on dangerous sports. You will have to guard against accidents associated with weapons or machinery. Impulsive financial speculation can lead to losses, and uncontrolled desires can lead to almost anything! A slipped disc is a strong likelihood with this progression and care should be taken to keep control of your temper and of your life.

Sun in challenging aspect to Jupiter

This can lead to arrogance, intolerance and an exaggerated idea of your own importance. There may be too much expansion in some area of your life and you could go totally over the top in anything from a philosophical belief to a business venture. Your attitude will be impractical and this will create problems in all your relationships with others. You may become extravagant or there may be unavoidable losses. Foreigners and foreign travel may prove difficult, as could legal or educational matters.

Sun in challenging aspect to Saturn

Personal ambition and creativity will be stifled for a while and everything will be just that bit harder to achieve. Social life and romance will probably disappear, and illness or depression could limit your activities for a while. You may become cold, hard and rigid in your opinions and you may try to use your position and status in order to push others around. You will find it hard to gain recognition and even harder to find love. Children may be a burden to you at this time, and children themselves who are under this progression will feel unloved.

Sun in challenging aspect to Uranus

Your behaviour could become completely incomprehensible under this transit and you may vacillate between one kind of belief and another. Nobody will be able to work out what you are going to do next. You will find life unpredictable and unsettled for a while and you may end the transit or progression by changing your way of life forever. Restlessness and eccentricity will drive you to break out of your rut and make changes. There will be changes in connection with friends and also with children at this time. You may leave a group of people with whom you have been associated for some time past or you may decide to join a new and different group of people now.

Sun in challenging aspect to Neptune

It will be hard to keep a grip on your life now. Partnerships may be extremely strange or ultimately disappointing. You must take care in business, romance and just about everything else that is important in life. You may overdo things in many ways, either by falling in love with the wrong person or by taking a real interest in drink or drugs. Delusions of grandeur or any other false illusions could make you hard to fathom. You may become quite psychic, especially in connection with dreams. Avoid medical treatments if you can and be very careful about any medication that you take. Children may drive you crazy at this time. Take care whom you trust.

Sun in challenging aspect to Pluto

You will have to take care in all business dealings and also in connection with taxes, legal matters, corporate matters and other people's money. Guard against becoming involved in power struggles at work or in sexual relationships. Sex, birth, death and all the deeper aspects of life could cause you problems. You will have to make some kind of transformation to your life style, but this may work out well in the end.

Sun in challenging aspect to Chiron

Watch your health and also the health of those who are around you. You may want to teach others how to live, only to find that they don't want to listen. Relationships and work could cause problems for a while. You may be restricted in some way now.

Sun in challenging aspect to the nodes

It may be hard to get the world to accept your ideas and your personality could be stepped on by others. Family life will be difficult and anything domestic will be a bit awkward too. There may be some kind of karmic debt to be paid.

Sun in challenging aspect to the ascendant

There could be problems with children or with creative projects. Guard against becoming egotistical.

Sun in challenging aspect to the midheaven

Problems associated with authority figures could feature now and your own authority will be challenged. It will be hard to achieve your objectives for a while.

22

The Moon in Detail

IF YOU GAIN nothing else from this book, do make sure that you learn how to read the progressed Moon, because this gives such a marvellous picture of the circumstances through which a subject is living at any one time and, in particular, the things that are occupying their mind at the time of any reading. The aspects that the Moon makes by the day-for-a-year method are an excellent timing device.

Timescale

The Moon takes a touch less than two and a half years to progress through a sign (roughly a degree per month). If the equal house method is used, the Moon also takes two and a half years to pass through each house. If Placidus, Koch or any other system is used, the Moon could take anything from less than a year to about four years to pass through a house.

A lunar transit will pass by in a matter of hours, but this can be extremely useful when looking at a very critical event that occurs at a specific time. Typical examples would be signing a contract, attending a job interview or making an important phone call.

Correspondences

The fourth house and Cancer.

The body

The lungs, breasts, rib cage, stomach and digestive organs, the alimentary canal, sternum, womb and pancreas.

Character

The Moon refers to personal and inner emotional matters, and also to the atmosphere closely surrounding the subject. Domestic and family circumstances become important and the subject will be forced to make an evaluation of everything that is dear to their heart. Petty and unimportant matters may take on a great significance for a while and then subside quickly once the progression has passed. Mothers, motherhood and women in general are ruled by the Moon, as are a whole collection of strange things, such as dealing with the public, travel and restlessness, health matters – especially those brought on by stress – and also some real oddities like sailors, as well as sewing, cooking and all the equipment that these things entail.

When you look back over your life you will notice that certain situations frequently last for two and a half years. Obviously five, seven and a half or ten-year periods become important too. In addition to these lunar phases, Saturn also takes two and a half years to make a transit across a sign or house, and this helps to stamp the character of each of these periods on a subject's consciousness.

When the Moon aspects a planet or an angle, in addition to emphasizing its own character, it also brings out the character of whatever is being aspected. The Moon tends to reflect the energies from the other features on the chart rather than stamping its own nature on them. Therefore the emotional response from a Moon square Mars situation would be very different from a Moon trine Jupiter, even though the Moon is involved in both types of aspect. It really does act as a kind of trigger. The sign and house that the Moon is in at the time of a reading offers an accurate barometer of the subject's feelings and life style.

Elements and qualities

Because the progressed Moon is so vitally important, I want to encourage you to reach for the feeling behind each progression. Therefore, look back over your own chart (and also those of your loved ones) and see how you felt when the Moon was in an earth sign, a mutable sign or an angular house. The following ideas may help you.

The elements

The Moon is associated with the water sign of Cancer and also with the sea because the ancients thought that it disappeared beneath the ocean during the hours of daylight and also during the dark of the Moon. Cancer is, of course, ruled by the Moon, while another water sign, Pisces, is ruled by the god of the oceans, Neptune. The third water sign, Scorpio, is out on a bit of a limb, because it is associated with the scorpion or, in ancient times, the eagle. Scorpions don't all live in the desert, but they don't dwell in watery areas. When the Moon is traversing a water sign, you can expect emotional, relationship, domestic and family matters to come to the fore.

Fire signs are aligned to the Sun and the 'hot' planets of Mars and Jupiter, which makes them a most hostile environment for the goddess of the seas. The progression of the Moon across a fire sign will bring feelings to the surface. Sexual and emotional situations can trigger off furious bouts of rage or of passion. However, there is an added level of energy here which can make a person more courageous and inclined to get new ideas off the ground.

Earth signs suit the Moon quite well and may actually help to calm the emotions. Steady progress and financial benefits can be made when the Moon is crossing an earth sign, but feelings of jealousy and possessiveness may surface.

Air signs are not particularly comfortable for the Moon to traverse because they rely on logic rather than emotions. The outcome of the Moon's voyage across an air sign could set up the kind of irritated response that Mr Spock is likely to display when asked to explain his feelings!

Qualities

The Moon is associated with the cardinal sign of Cancer, so it is probably happiest in any of the cardinal signs. A fixed sign is at odds with the restless nature of the Moon, while a mutable sign might dissipate some of its energies.

Houses

Angular houses: first, fourth, seventh, tenth

The Moon will trigger off major changes when it traverses an angular house. In the first the ego must come to the fore. In the fourth the home and family may go through changes. In the seventh partnerships become an issue, and in the tenth changes in goals and objectives occur.

Succedent houses: second, fifth, eighth, eleventh

Things settle down a bit when the Moon is in one of these houses. Consolidation rather than change will be the name of the game. Any changes that occur will be harder to bear at this time.

Mutable houses: third, sixth, ninth, twelfth

The Moon is considered to be a restless planet and these are considered to be restless houses, so travel, either locally or overseas, becomes important. You may bring certain aspects of your life to a close when the Moon is in these houses, in preparation for the new beginnings that the cardinal houses are likely to bring. As your moon progresses through a sign and house, you will draw towards you people who are of a similar type. Thus a progressed Moon through Sagittarius and the sixth house will bring you into contact with Sagittarian or Virgoan types.

The Moon through Aries or the first house

This is a time of rebirth. You will be forced to abandon old ways of life and to look around for something new. You will feel more passionate about everything and, even if you are normally placid, you will be more enthusiastic and excited about life. The ego comes to the fore and you begin to demand more out of life for yourself. This can lead to conflicts with others, especially with other family members, authority figures and those who seek to restrict you. The emotions rise to the surface, making you more susceptible to love and passion and also to moody feelings and a general dissatisfaction with your past way of life. Your rather raw and tender feelings will be a contributory factor in family arguments at this time. You may have to deal with females in the family in quite a serious manner. Familiar patterns of life begin to break up.

In working life there will be new contacts, new ideas and many short-term schemes. New ways of working can occur at this time. Travel or a connection with the sea are possible now. You will be more self-centred, more inclined to look after your own needs rather than those of others. Your sex drive will increase and this may also contribute to a change of partnerships. Even if you don't change partners, a move of house and new family groupings and arrangements are likely to happen to you. You will be less able to put up with the limits that your previous life style has set upon you.

Summary

- New beginnings, new outlook
- More egotistical and self-centred
- Change of address
- More passionate
- Problems with or over women
- Need for a new way of working

The Moon through Taurus or the second house

This is the start of a more settled and comfortable phase in which projects that were enthusiastically undertaken in Aries are put into steady action. Material matters become important now and you will make a start on getting a nice home together or buying land that you can grow things on. You will begin to make and keep money at this time, and any goods that you buy now will be durable. You will become reluctant to lend or waste money, and speculative ventures will hold no interest for you. Anything that you begin now will be meant to last. This is a good time to form business partnerships, especially with women, and these too will last. Emotional partnerships should also be much more durable, but they lack intensity and passion and you will be happier to found a stable family than to flit from lover to lover. You will become keen on art, music, dancing, photography and anything else that has a connection to form and beauty. Building, gardening, cookery, decorating your home and other such creative interests will hold your interest.

Summary

- A need for permanence
- A desire for money and goods
- A desire to create beauty

The Moon through Gemini or the third house

Perpetual motion is the message of this sign and house. You will be more restless than before and you will probably pack as much as you can into your life just to keep yourself from becoming bored. This is a time for mental exploration and you have an urge to educate yourself. You would be particularly keen to communicate with others and you may begin to use such skills in a job of work. This could lead you into office work, sales, teaching and other forms of communication. Temporary work, short-term jobs or work that takes you around from place to place are all possible now.

Local issues will become part of your life and you could get together with friends and neighbours in order to improve your area, or to raise funds for a local school. You can expect plenty of visits to places of local interest and also several people coming to visit you at your home. Love and romance may be put on the back burner for the time being, because you will be more interested in improving your mental processes than your love life. However, connections with intelligent and interesting people could enhance your personal life. You may flirt more and be less inclined to stick faithfully to the same old partner. Your emotions may confuse you because they will get in the way of logic and clarity of perception.

Summary

- Restlessness and changeability
- Interest in communications
- Desire to learn or to pick up new skills
- Logic trying to override emotion
- Local travel and local interests
- Attachment to siblings and neighbours

The Moon through Cancer or the fourth house

The Moon is at its most comfortable in this sign or house, but that doesn't necessarily mean that your life is guaranteed to be happy throughout the whole progression. For one thing, you may be more moody and prone to greater emotional highs and lows. It may be hard for you to understand your own feelings at times. The past will draw your attention and you may take an interest in history or in collecting things that have a history attached to them. You may bore your family and friends by frequently referring to things that happened in the past.

Family life comes to the fore under this progression and you may set up a home and a family now. A change of address is possible or, perhaps, the acquisition of a shop or some other kind of premises. You may become attached to someone else's home for a while. Feelings of family loyalty become stronger and you may fancy researching your family tree. The need to identify with a particular group, race or religion will exert a powerful tug. You may retreat from the world and immerse yourself in domesticity, or, alternatively, you could begin to run a small business from your home. Your intuitive and psychic abilities will come to the fore. Your emotions will bring periods of jealousy, possessiveness and loneliness, even when these emotions are unfounded. You may want to be alone and yet fear being lonely. In a lighter vein, you will seek out novelties by visiting new places, especially those with a history to them, and travel will become more important to you.

Summary

- Desire for a home or other premises
- Need for family life
- Closeness and interaction with women
- Travel
- Emotional attachment to the past

Moon through Leo or the fifth house

This progression should bring you into contact with babies, children or young people. There could be babies born into your circle or you may take up a job or hobby in connection with children or young people. Your own behaviour will become more playful and childlike and you will begin to look around for pastimes and hobbies that allow you to play. Creativity is the watchword now and this need will energize you into creating something important. You may write the definitive novel or produce a painting to rival that of the great masters, but it could just as easily be the establishment of a home, a family or a worthy cause that occupies your attention. Creative hobbies will appeal to you now because an artistic outlet will be a necessity. You also need the attention that creative success will bring you.

You will become bored with mundane jobs and begin to seek work with a touch of glamour about it. Your optimistic attitude could lead you to open your own business. You need to be somebody that people notice and your light cannot now be hidden under a bushel. Your feelings will rise to the surface and they may be hard to control. If you have spent your life thus far being kept down, your oppressors are in for a surprise or two. Exciting love affairs may become a feature of your life now, especially if you have been putting up with a dull or meaningless partnership. You will need an outlet for your passions.

Summary

- Interest in children
- Need for a creative outlet
- Need for glamour

- Need for attention and adulation
- May be more easily irritated
- Need for passionate outlet

Moon through Virgo or the sixth house

This is a great time to take up a new career because all forms of work will prosper now. This is especially so if the job is analytical in nature and/or if it concerns communications or the medical field. Book-keeping, record-keeping and office equipment could become an important feature of your life now. Do-it-yourself work, dress-making or any other creative craft that requires dexterity and concentration would succeed at this time, as would writing. You may take up farming or gardening. This is a good time to establish sensible work habits and also to employ staff to help you cope. You may take up some form of training in order to brush up your skills, and even if you don't you are sure to learn much that will be useful to you in the future. Your mind will become sharper and so will your sense of humour.

You may become interested in health and healing, either of the normal medical variety or in the alternative therapy field. There may be an attachment to clinics, hospitals or doctors' surgeries due to family health problems or to finding a job in such a place. You will have to avoid taking on too much and working so hard that your nerves become stretched. You may become faddy about food. Guilty feelings may plague you and you could become far too critical of yourself and others. Working relationships are more likely to be formed than personal ones. One rather nice compensatory factor for this all-work-and-no-play syndrome is that it is a favourable time to buy yourself new clothes.

Summary

- Traditionally this progression rules employers, employees and servants
- Duty
- Work, especially detailed analytical tasks
- Crafts and hobbies
- Health and healing

- Food and farming
- New clothing

Moon through Libra or the seventh house

Partnerships and relationships are the most significant feature of this progression, and you will split away from some of those people who have been a feature of your life up to now and form business or personal partnerships. Your emotions will be strong and often at odds with each other, possibly requiring security and freedom at the same time. To be honest, this progression is better used for exploring new relationships than for outright commitment, except in the business sphere, when it works very well. This is an excellent time for all forms of business, especially where you have to act as an agent or assure that fair play is the rule. You will take care of your appearance and generally behave in an attractive and pleasant manner both at work and in your personal life. Legal matters may need to be attended to at this time, especially partnership agreements. This should be a happy time when you achieve a balance in everything.

Summary

- Partnerships of all kinds
- Legal matters
- Balanced outlook

The Moon through Scorpio or the eighth house

This progression brings crucial events because it is associated with the most vital aspects of life. There will be children born into your circle and also possible deaths among your group. This is a time when one moves up a generation, perhaps becoming a parent while one's own grandparents die off. Any form of separation, divorce and other losses will be compensated for by forming new relationships with other people as time goes by. Business relationships that tie you financially will be formed now and other people's financial situations will become interesting. There will be dealings with the legal and official aspects of money and business in the forms of mortgages, taxation, legacies and corporate matters of all kinds. There may be legal wrangles over property or goods relating to partnerships that have ended. You could set up a new home or place of business with someone new, and, fortunately, there are great opportunities opening up for money-making.

Investigations will become important, and these may take the form of medical examinations, police or other detective-type enquiries, insurances, or even the search for oil, gold or anything else that is hidden. Psychic and mystical matters may interest you and your level of intuition will increase. This is likely to be a very stressful time for both positive and negative reasons, and you will end this period feeling wrung out by the course of events that you live through. However, you will probably get your life into a new and better order as a result. You should make some really good financial gains during this period.

Summary

- Major changes through births, deaths and partnerships
- Legal and property matters
- Business and tax matters
- Financial changes leading to gains

Moon through Sagittarius or the ninth house

This progression will bring a great expansion in all your horizons. Far-away places and the people who come from them will become a feature of your life now. This could take you travelling to places that you had never thought you would see. Foreigners, foreign goods and ideas that emerge from cultures and backgrounds that are different from yours will become important. You may choose to live in another country for a while and also to learn another language. You could fall in love with a foreigner. This may lead you to investigate religions and philosophies that are different from yours. You may decide to take up some form of higher education, and the subject you choose could well have a philosophical aspect to it. There may be more contact with schools, colleges and churches as part of your daily life. Another possibility is of contact with the law and legal institutions. Legal matters could become an important part of your life now.

There should be a lot more fun in your life under this progression. You make take up hobbies and pastimes or become enthusiastic about sports. Sagittarius is traditionally associated with horses, so you may just learn to ride or to put a complicated bet on at the races! You may become more than usually interested in such spiritual concepts as mediumship, spiritual healing, reincarnation and even astrology! Your values will become more spiritual and less materialistic and your sense of humour will become sharper. You will need to guard against overoptimism or expanding your horizons too quickly.

Summary

- An interest in foreigners and/or foreign goods
- Spiritual matters become important
- Attachment to churches, schools or similar places
- Higher education
- The law and legal matters
- Gambling, horses, fun, humour and amusements

The Moon through Capricorn or the tenth house

You will work hard while the Moon is in this sign or house and there will be a number of large and fairly prestigious projects for you to complete. Details will need attention and you may feel at times as though you are being overwhelmed by work and responsibilities. You may suffer one or two setbacks and some sphere of your life may become limited or restricted. A chronic ailment may surface and you could feel very old and tired at times. Older people or those in positions of authority will do much to help you reach your goals, and in the end all the hard work will have been worth it. It will be easy for you to sell a product or a service at this time. You will learn how to work in a structured and businesslike manner. Your work could bring you into contact with the public. You will take a sensitive attitude towards colleagues and employees.

Personal and business relationships will become blurred and you may begin to work with someone you love or, alternatively, fall in love with a person you meet through your work. This is not a truly romantic time, however, and your feelings may need to be kept under tight control. It may not be possible to be with the one you love as much as you would like. Domestic life will take a back seat and you could leave this in the hands of others while you concentrate on your career. Parents, older people and authority figures will become an important feature of your life now. You could become a grandparent yourself under this progression! Your attitude will be quite materialistic at this time. Guard against becoming hard and calculating or working yourself into the ground.

Summary

- A time for work and advancement
- Attention to detail
- Success after great effort
- Older people, parents and authority figures become important
- Work and personal relationships merge
- Illness or some other limitation possible

The Moon through Aquarius or the eleventh house

Friends will become an important feature of your life at this time and you will have more dealings with other people than formerly. You will feel the need to be identified with a particular group of people who share your views and represent a life style to which you aspire. There may be a cause or a movement that attracts you now. At work, you will have to perform either as part of a team or in charge of a group, and you will not be able to achieve too much on your own at this time. You will strive for independence and you could seek to leave a situation that you see as being repressive or non-fulfilling. There will be contact with helpful women now but there could also be differences of opinion. The urge to learn new things will lead you to seek education or to gain new skills. Modern methods and electronic equipment will begin to fascinate you. If you don't own a computer, this is the time when you will acquire one.

You will redefine your hopes and wishes and you may seek a completely different direction to the one you have followed up to now. Guard against becoming destructive, irrational or eccentric at this time and try not to push away all those who love you. The chances are that the situation you are in at the start of the progression will change radically by the time you end it. During this two-and-a-half-year period, you could change job, move house, change your life style, fall in love with someone really 'different' and leave your partner! Radical change cannot be avoided.

Summary

- Group or team activities will attract
- Education or training probable
- Independent, stubborn and pugnacious attitude possible
- Friends become important
- Drastic change of life style

The Moon through Pisces or the twelfth house

This will be a time of reflection and retreat from life. You may feel like a hermit at times, either staying quietly at home, living alone, working from home or simply not feeling much like being sociable. You will become kinder and nicer but also more vulnerable. Your own personality may have to be suppressed for a while for the sake of others or for the common good. You will become involved with secrets of some kind. One such possibility could be of setting up a small business on the quiet while still working for someone else. There could be any amount of secret romantic entanglements or you may be accused of doing something that you have not done. Your family may find an excuse to exclude you from the fold. You must strive to keep hold of reality now and not find yourself falling into a strange emotional morass. Try to avoid drink, drugs and opiates if you can. There may be a connection to hospitals, prisons or places of seclusion for a while. You may even begin to work in one of these.

On the positive side, you can learn to relax and enjoy a quieter and more reflective life style. You may travel to the sea or even move near water. Artistic and creative skills will develop and you could learn to become quite competent at something such as dress-making or film- and video-making. Metaphysical and psychic concepts will begin to interest you now and you could develop a genuine flair for something interesting, such as reading the runes. You will notice a great increase in your intuitive perception and probably real flashes of ESP at times. Strange and unconscious forces could almost possess you occasionally and, if you are really unlucky, you could fall into an obsessive and devastating love affair. Aim to keep your head from slipping right off your shoulders if you can and try not to become the architect of your own undoing with this progression.

Summary

- Seclusion and reflection, possibly living alone
- Attachment to prisons, hospitals or other places of seclusion
- Interest in psychic matters and increase of psychic intuition
- Travel to or over water
- Secrets and possible exclusion from family life
- Kindness and vulnerability

23

The Progressed Moon and the Decanates

IN CHAPTER 17 we took a look at the decans or decanates. To recap the theory, each sign is divided into three ten-degree decanates; the first of these is sub-ruled by the sign itself, the second is sub-ruled by the next sign along *in the same element*, and the third is sub-ruled by the final sign *in the same element*. For example, the first decanate of Aries is sub-ruled by Aries, the second by Leo and the third by Sagittarius, all of these being signs of the fire element.

Because the Moon moves so quickly, it traverses a whole decanate in just under a year, thus adding an interesting touch of spice to any lunar progression. The following 'cookbook' list is far from deep or comprehensive, but it will give you an idea of what to look out for.

It is interesting to note that the first decanate of any sign is always sub-ruled by *itself*, so it is obviously at its most effective. Perhaps this is a necessity, because if it were not so the ingress of a planet into a new sign wouldn't make as much of an impression. As the Moon works through the decanates of any sign the effect of the sub-rulers becomes quite obvious.

Progressed Moon through Aries

Aries/Aries

Pure Aries: all the Arian traits are emphasized.

Aries/Leo

You will develop a more settled and steady attitude that helps you finish whatever you start. There is a need for drama in life and for attention. An interest in children, creativity, glamour, leisure pursuits, holidays and love affairs is evident.

Aries/Sagittarius

The common sense of the Leo decanate departs and a rather scatty attitude begins to take hold. Ideas and enthusiasms fill your mind but you may find it hard to stick to anything. Interests and involvements could include travel, contact with foreigners or foreign goods, legal matters, higher education, religion, philosophy and spiritual matters.

Progressed Moon through Taurus

Taurus/Taurus

Pure Taurus: all the Taurean traits are emphasized.

Taurus/Virgo

You will be brighter and quicker under this progression and there may be an emphasis on duty, employment and health. Food, farming and communications become more important.

Taurus/Capricorn

A more businesslike and practical attitude will possess you now and you could really work very hard both for money and for increased status. There will be an interest in big business, banking and anything that helps you reach your goals. You will concentrate on details.

Progressed Moon through Gemini

Gemini/Gemini

Pure Gemini: all the Geminian traits are emphasized.

Gemini/Libra

This is a calmer phase with the emphasis on heart-to-heart communication. You may become more streetwise and more up-to-date. Liaison jobs, partnerships and a desire for a peaceful life will appeal.

Gemini/Aquarius

This progression will open your eyes to many new possibilities. You will begin to break out of your mould and to make some important changes. You will also become more dispassionate. You could become involved with humanitarian issues, education, astrology and politics.

Progressed Moon through Cancer

Cancer/Cancer

Pure Cancer: all the Cancerian traits are emphasized.

Cancer/Scorpio

Your emotions will become more intense and relationship matters will mean more to you. Sex could become an issue now. You may get the urge to investigate certain matters, and all the Scorpio interests of health, psychic matters and major life events will become important.

Cancer/Pisces

You will become kinder and less dogmatic now. Mysteries will interest you and you may become involved with psychic matters. You may be more emotional and chaotic and less in control of your life. You could become interested in helping people who are in seclusion or you could find yourself hiding away from the world for a while.

Progressed Moon through Leo

Leo/Leo

Pure Leo: all the Leonine traits are emphasized.

Leo/Sagittarius

The rather heavy and dramatic Leonine attitude will ease and a great sense of humour will begin to develop. Look back to the Sagittarian interests in the Aries/Sagittarius section.

Leo/Aries

This combination gives a real thrust for power and achievement. Your ego will come to the fore and you may begin to move so quickly that others cannot see you for dust. The Aries interests of big military-type organizations may begin to appeal, as might engineering, education and the cutting edge of business.

Progressed Moon through Virgo

Virgo/Virgo

Pure Virgo: all the Virgoan traits are emphasized.

Virgo/Capricorn

This leads to an interest in goals and achievement. There may be an attachment to older people and a sense of obligation towards them. Check back to Taurus/Capricorn to find more of these traits.

Virgo/Taurus

There will be a practical approach to goods and money. You may grow calmer, quieter and more thorough. You will become happier and more sociable and as interested in the quality of life as you are in the quantity of it. Money will be easier to make and keep.

Progressed Moon through Libra

Libra/Libra

Pure Libra: all the Libran traits are emphasized.

Libra/Aquarius

You will become less practical and more excitable. There could be an interest in Aquarian subjects (see Gemini/Aquarius). You will want to stretch your intellect and you could take up the law or politics or work for a trades union.

Libra/Gemini

You will become more streetwise and more up-to-date under

this progression. You may also become a little superficial, with a little knowledge about everything but not too much about anything. Any indecisiveness from which you normally suffer will increase a little.

Progressed Moon through Scorpio

Scorpio/Scorpio
Pure Scorpio: all the Scorpionic traits are emphasized.

Scorpio/Pisces
Any interest in psychic matters will increase. You will still be moody and emotional but more inclined to see the other person's point of view. You could become quite vulnerable. (See also Cancer/Pisces for more information.)

Scorpio/Cancer
You will become more home-loving and quite keen to nurture those who are around you. There may be an attachment to female family members and the domestic scene will interest you more. You may become interested in genealogy, collecting or history, especially the history of warfare. You may move house or create a new family unit.

Progressed Moon through Sagittarius

Sagittarius/Sagittarius
Pure Sagittarius: all the Sagittarian traits are emphasized.

Sagittarius/Aries
This fiery combination will really get you moving. Mundane life will hold no interest for you, so you will begin to become interested in fresh ideas and new people all around. (Check Aries/Sagittarius for more ideas.)

Sagittarius/Leo
This progression will have a calming effect but it will also increase your desire to make something of yourself. You will need to be the centre of attention and require life to be more

dramatic and important for a while. (See Aries/Leo for more.)

Progressed Moon through Capricorn

Capricorn/Capricorn

Pure Capricorn: all the Capricornian traits are emphasized.

Capricorn/Taurus

This is a good money-making combination and a practical attitude to money and possessions will be needed. You may become more interested in creative or artistic hobbies and pastimes. (See also Taurus/Capricorn.)

Capricorn/Virgo

This makes for a hard-working phase with an emphasis on employers, employees, duties and communications work. Health, food fads and the need to look after others are also probable.

Progressed Moon through Aquarius

Aquarius/Aquarius

Pure Aquarius: all the Aquarian traits are emphasized.

Aquarius/Gemini

This adds ambition and business success to the proliferation of Aquarian ideas. A mixture of pragmatism and idealism will abound. You will be more interested in teaching and training. (See also Gemini/Aquarius.)

Aquarius/Libra

This adds a calmer and more cooperative attitude to the Aquarian idealism. You will want to coexist with others in a harmonious atmosphere. Business and personal partnerships could take off now. (See also Libra/Aquarius for more.)

Progressed Moon through Pisces

Pisces/Pisces
Pure Pisces: all the Piscean traits are emphasized.

Pisces/Cancer
You will be kind and helpful to others but you may be too ready to make a martyr of yourself. Family life will predominate and you may be happy to stay in or near home, surrounded by your loved ones. Travel on, by or over water is possible now. (See Cancer/Pisces for more.)

Pisces/Scorpio
This adds a sharpness to your outlook and you will want to delve beneath the surface of everything that is going on around you. Your moods could become quite explosive at times. (See Scorpio/Pisces for more information.)

24

Lunar Aspects

WHEN DOING day-for-a-year progressions, these lunar aspects assume a terrific importance. In fact, coupled with transits, this is probably the most accurate and interesting form of predictive astrology that there is. Each progression will last for about a month but it can have a tremendous and lasting impact on your life. Lunar aspects are the triggers of your life, setting off trains of events that are fascinating to watch and to live through.

Moon in happy aspect to natal Moon

This would be a good time to change your address or to invest in property. Family matters will go well, as will anything that involves women or women's interests. You may be emotional and rather restless at this time, so take a journey or two, because travel is well aspected now.

Moon in happy aspect to Mercury

Your curiosity will be stimulated by this progression, and the harnessing of your imagination to your intellect could have very interesting results. Travel around your locality will be well starred now. Business matters, especially those that require negotiation, trading or communication, will go well. This is a good time to enjoy sporting activities, and also the company of younger people.

Moon in happy aspect to Venus

This is a wonderful time to fall in love! But be careful, because your feelings are vulnerable and close to the surface now. There may be family celebrations and happy events of all kinds, especially those that bring you into contact with others in a social setting. Holidays, nice dinners and other outings will please you. You may become involved in something to do with music, beauty or other pleasant subjects. Your financial situation should improve but you may also be in a mood to spend money, and, if so, you will buy goods that are attractive, lasting and a little luxurious.

Moon in happy aspect to Mars

This aspect will heighten your feelings and it may make you rash or impetuous. You will find it hard to keep your temper and you may fly off the handle all too easily. It would be best to take your time over any important decisions. Dealings with men will be very interesting and, due to the passion of the planets involved, this can mark the start of an important love affair. Family and domestic matters should go well but your impatient attitude may make you irritable towards those who are close to you.

Moon in happy aspect to Jupiter

This is a good aspect if you want to deal with property or premises. A change of address or any major refurbishments would go well. Legal matters related to property or the family would also succeed. You may become involved in religious or spiritual matters, possibly through coming into contact with interesting new people who introduce you to new concepts. This is a good time to learn or to teach, and if you need to take an examination you should be successful in your endeavours. Finances should pick up and there should be some excellent business opportunities, with such matters as publishing or broadcasting being especially successful. Foreigners, foreign travel or anything to do with foreign goods are well starred. Most of your schemes should succeed at this lucky time.

However, a Moon/Jupiter conjunction can bring losses in one area while bringing gains in another.

Moon in happy aspect to Saturn

Saturn being the gloomy planet that it is, even a good aspect can be something of a downer. This will heap a certain amount of extra responsibility onto your shoulders and it may be a time of very hard work. You could be a bit off colour at this time or just tired and feeling that you are being overworked and underpaid. However, you will finish all that you start now and you will be well rewarded for anything that you do. This is an excellent time in which to deal with those in authority over you and also to sort out anything regarding older relatives. Your own authority and status should improve. You must pay some extra attention to the home and to your family at this time and you will also take a serious attitude to any domestic problems that you find yourself faced with. Your emotions will be under control and you shouldn't be swept away by your feelings.

Moon in happy aspect to Uranus

Uranus always brings the unexpected but at least the surprises should be pleasant ones. This should convey good news in connection with family and domestic matters and it could bring unexpected visitors or an opportunity to visit other people in their homes. You will make new friends and you could also join a group or an organization that looks like being fun. Any business that concerns food, women's interests or domestic matters will go well. You may be a bit overemotional and overexcited at times, but so what? Enjoy it!

Moon in happy aspect to Neptune

You will become a really sensitive soul under this progression because Neptune will make you compassionate towards the sufferings of others. You may want to do something for the plight of the homeless or of suffering animals, or similar work. Artistic and creative endeavours will do well and you could become keen on photography, poetry, music or anything else that evokes memories and feelings. You may find yourself looking back over your past and even reliving something that happened to you years ago. You will become more receptive to your inner feelings and you will notice an increase in your intuitive powers. Precognitive dreams are possible at this time. Day dreams are also possible and you may lose yourself in a time of dreaming and drifting for a while. Perhaps you need the rest.

Moon in happy aspect to Pluto

This is going to bring a transformation to your life. You may decide to move house or to change your domestic circumstances in some way. If this occurs when other important progressions or transits happen, it could be life changing. If this is the only progression, it will still bring some crucial concerns to a head. Important matters relating to births, deaths, beginnings and endings can go your way, and if you have to deal with legacies, taxes and other joint affairs these should prosper now. Your sex life may suddenly pick up, and both secret and open liaisons are likely to move into a more passionate phase.

This can be a subterranean time where more may go on in your mind and your heart than out in the world in a very obvious way. This is a good aspect for business matters, especially those that involve shared finances, and if you happen to be in business with a partner or a spouse this should bring advantages. There may be karmic benefits due to the good things that you have done for others in the past. You may become more than usually interested in psychic subjects, but there could just as easily be an increased attraction to such things as police or medical matters. Any dealings that you have with the general public will go well and you may be able to influence people in a beneficial way. This is a good time to recycle things and to make something new out of something old. You may also find things that you mislaid years ago. Something will turn up, that's for sure.

Moon in happy aspect to Chiron

If you or anybody close to you has been ill lately, the situation should begin to improve rapidly. Your compassion for those who need help will be stimulated at this time. There could be some kind of strangely karmic or emotionally important event in your life, and you could learn a lot from this. Matters of freedom or restriction will come to the fore.

Moon in happy aspect to the nodes

This is likely to bring joy and happiness on the domestic front. Business matters may go well and there may be a karmic feeling to everything that is going on. If you deal with the public, this too will be a success.

Moon in happy aspect to the ascendant

Happy family life and a good mood all around you characterize this event. You will feel optimistic and outgoing and anything that you start now should go well in the future. Domestic and family matters are well starred, as are any business matters relating to farming, food, women's interests or the general public.

Moon in happy aspect to the midheaven

If you need to improve your image out in the world, this is the time to do it. Public relations and sales or marketing of any kind will succeed, as will domestic and family matters. This would be a good time to entertain important people at your place of work or in your home.

Moon in challenging aspect to the natal Moon

Domestic and family matters are likely to be strained just now and this is a bad time to call in the builders or to try to move house. Your emotions will be stretched and you may go down with some kind of ailment as a result of stress. Travel is not well starred, although you are restless enough to try it anyway.

Moon in challenging aspect to Mercury

The car may let you down, your local buses and trains will probably go on strike and your bike will spring a puncture. Your temper will not be at its best. Domestic matters will become screwed up and some piece of machinery that you depend upon may suddenly develop a bad case of the gremlins. Older women will get you down and business matters will be delayed or difficult. Your brothers or sisters could aggravate you.

Moon in challenging aspect to Venus

Partnerships will be difficult and a romance may suddenly go wrong. You may fall in love with someone totally unsuitable because your feelings are vulnerable and you may not be able to think straight. Family celebrations and events will be a source of irritation and anything to do with domestic life will be fraught. Don't buy anything important now if you can help it, especially if it is something for the home. Women will be a source of aggravation and your health may not be the best. There may be more work than play for a while, and even if you do make your mind up to go out and socialize, your partner, your friends and your colleagues won't want to. Try not to become involved in any business dealings or money transactions now if you can avoid it.

Moon in challenging aspect to Mars

To say you could lose your temper is understating the case, because you could go absolutely 'ballistic' at this time. Guard against accidents through rashness and do try to take your time over everything for a while. A man may drive you to distraction and any woman who is involved with a man in a personal way will be tempted to walk out. Hold on, this is only a phase and it will soon pass! Family matters will be extremely irritating, as will business matters for a while. Try to rid yourself of excess energy by taking the dog for a walk (that is, if the dog is still talking to you!) Try your hand at sports but avoid dangerous ones at this time. If in doubt, stay home, in bed, ALONE!

Moon in challenging aspect to Jupiter

This could be an expensive time with unexpected bills and few opportunities of finding any extra cash. Dealings that involve legal or property matters (or both) will be difficult to manage. Any business that involves farming, food, women's issues, publishing, broadcasting or the general public will be awkward. You may find that your beliefs are being challenged and you may temporarily lose faith in your guardian angels or in yourself. Educational matters will go slowly and you may 'plough' any exams that you have to take at this time. This is a poor time to travel or to deal with foreigners.

Moon in challenging aspect to Saturn

If a happy aspect to Saturn can feel like all work and no play, you can imagine what a challenging one feels like! This will be a time of hard, unremitting work and the rewards may not be obvious or quick to materialize. A chronic illness could suddenly assert itself and you would have to start to pay attention to this. People in positions of authority could be very hard on you and life in general is likely to be unfair and difficult for a while. Parents and older relatives will be awkward and demanding and family life may be depressing. You may long to move house or to do something about your surroundings but you could be short of the time, the money or the opportunity to do so. Alternatively, you may be up to your neck in builders and mess. Like all hard times, this too will pass and something else will take its place. Just learn to be patient and resilient and wait for better times to come. That is the lesson of Saturn, the teacher of the zodiac.

Moon in challenging aspect to Uranus

If you are into reading the tarot, this is rather like seeing the Struck Tower in a tarot reading. Shocks, surprises, revelations, upheavals and a totally unpredictable phase are in store for you now. The best side of this is that you will at least be aware of what has been going on and will no longer be kept in the dark. There could be sudden events in connection with your home and family or among your friends. If you have been involved in a group activity for some time, there will be sudden changes of direction that may leave you on the outside looking in. Nothing is certain now and your own mood is strangely rebellious, eccentric and awkward. You may want to make a bid for freedom and to cut all those ties that have become just a little too comfortable, familiar and boring. If other heavy aspects are involved, you will change your way of life quite dramatically.

Moon in challenging aspect to Neptune

Neptune being the vague planet that it is, this is a hard one to analyse. You may feel as though your life is on a kind roller-coaster, with the chief victim being your own emotions. The past could come back to haunt you in some way and you may have to face up to some pretty awful memories or feelings that have been buried for years. You will become oversensitive and terribly vulnerable, and if you are daft enough to fall in love at this time it could turn out to be a painful experience. However, with Neptune it is your unconscious and your dream life rather than anything really practical that is most likely to be attacked. This means that you may be able to live your life on the surface without making any real changes, while inside chaos reigns. Guard against deception in financial and business dealings and, if possible, leave any important decisions until well after this progression has passed. Artistic and creative ventures will be especially badly affected by this, so leave them alone.

Moon in challenging aspect to Pluto

This progression could change your life in a pretty big way, especially if there are other things going on in your chart at the same time. The chances are that the majority of changes will happen on a subconscious level or in your head rather than out in the open. You may find yourself facing up to something that, in your heart of hearts, you have known was wrong for a long time. You may bring an affair of the heart to an end or make a start on a new one, but, whichever way this goes, there will be pain and soul-searching on a deep inner level. You may suddenly become frightened by psychic experiences or by people who are sinister in some way. This is a poor time to get involved in business or partnership matters that involve shared resources. Legal and official matters can bring problems now and there could be family wrangles over wills, tax bills and so on. This is a poor time to buy property or to have major work done in your home. Family life is likely to be a bit tense. Your sex life could become an issue and this too could lead you to take some difficult decisions. Matters related to births, deaths, beginnings and endings may bring problems. It is a difficult time but, like all these progressions, it won't last forever – although it may feel like it.

Moon in challenging aspect to Chiron

This could bring health problems for you or yours. If you work in the health or healing field, things could be tough for a while. Teaching or learning could present difficulties, although this could turn out well in the end. You may feel as if you are going through the mill in a practical way, and your emotions may be a bit close to the surface now too. You may feel restricted for a while.

Moon in challenging aspect to the nodes

This is a really awkward one because the nodes represent sensitive areas in the path of the Moon. Therefore all the lunar problems of home, family, premises, food and farming, women's issues and public life could be adversely affected. There is usually a time and a place for everything, and just at the moment there seems to be a time and place for nothing. Your mother or other older relatives could be very demanding now and your mood is not a happy one. There may be some kind of karmic debt to be paid now.

Moon in challenging aspect to the ascendant

Logic and intuition will be at odds with each other and what feels right may not make sense, while the things that seem sensible won't feel right! You won't relate well to others and you may not understand yourself either for a while. This is not a great time for business, domestic life or matters of the heart.

Moon in challenging aspect to the midheaven

This aspect will bring difficulties in connection with your aims and ambitions. Business matters will not go well and there could be a conflict between your work and your home, with plenty of pressure coming at you from both sides. Your parents may not approve of what you are trying to do. This is a difficult time for real-estate transactions or for working in anything that is supplied to women or which deals with the public.

25

The Planets through the Houses

THE EASIEST WAY to deal with this is to consider the meanings of the houses and the effects of the planets on them as they pass through them. Until you find books that go into this in fuller detail, just keep the following key ideas in your mind. This section will be far less important when dealing with the day-for-a-year progressions than it would be for any other kind.

First house

Mercury

There will be new ideas and an interest in literature, communications and local travel.

Venus

This is a great time for social life, holidays and pleasure. You may become interested in music, beauty and art. Gifts could come your way now. Women will become important to some, as would money and the pleasure of spending it. You could fall in love.

Mars

An increase in energy and enterprise is possible, but your temper will be shorter. Men will be important and any love affairs will be passionate.

Jupiter

Travel and expansion of your horizons are likely. You may look for something new to believe in. New opportunities for money-making and new friends will enter your life now.

Saturn

This is a time of extra responsibility, but you will take this on willingly. Hard work brings rewards and older people may help you. You will have to watch your health.

Uranus

You will break out of your mould and do something *different*! Friends and group activities become important.

Neptune

Love and beauty enter your life and these could inspire you and make you more creative. You will become more sensitive, and if you have mediumistic tendencies these will increase. Guard against drawing losers to you or making unnecessary sacrifices.

Pluto

Pluto heralds major change, but it may be slow in coming. In some ways this is more a change of heart than a change of life. There is an increased connection to business, shared resources and such things as the police, the medical world and the occult.

Second house

Mercury

Money and business should be good and negotiations should go well. Travel in connection with business or to search out things that give you pleasure. Be careful with what you say and what you sign.

Venus

Females will be helpful and so-called women's interests will succeed. This is a good time for finances and also for sensible spending.

Mars
You will have plenty of energy for new money-making projects. You could value activities more than possessions now.

Jupiter
Valuable experiences will be gained through travel, expansion, foreigners and new business opportunities. There will also be openings to make or win money, but overexpansion must be avoided.

Saturn
You will be short of money and life could be hard but the outcome of any effort that you make should be beneficial.

Uranus
There will be ups and downs in financial matters and unusual sources of income. You may decide to change your outlook completely.

Neptune
If money is to be made, it will be through artistic or creative endeavours. You may lose or give away possessions, taking up some other value system than the material one.

Pluto
This could make you very rich and could change your outlook over a period of time. Sex could become an important issue.

Third house

Mercury
This is a great time for communications and for having an active mind. Don't wear your nerves out by thinking *too* much! Try to finish one task before starting another.

Venus
Good relationships with those who are around you and a peaceful frame of mind are likely. A good old gossip with a woman friend from time to time will perk you up. Socializing

with neighbours and siblings will be pleasant.

Mars

Guard against accidents while travelling because there will be an increase in the number of trips you have to take. Neighbours and siblings could be very helpful or a source of aggravation. You may be extremely articulate but also cutting at times.

Jupiter

This is a great time to ask for a raise or take a trip. Business and negotiations will go well.

Saturn

Guard against depression and try not to work too hard. Business matters should go well and steady progress can be made. You will make an effort to get on with those around you.

Uranus

Life could take off with a jolt now and an unsettled time is on the cards. Job changes, changes in the way you get around and a clutch of new faces will be part of your life now.

Neptune

You may write the definitive novel but you could also become quite upset by awful dreams and premonitions.

Pluto

You may try to influence the way the world thinks and you could even achieve this.

Fourth house

Mercury

This is a good time to buy or sell property or premises. Talks with family members will go well, and these could be on a reminiscent theme. Protect your home from thieves.

Venus

This is another good time to buy and sell property or premises, or to deal financially with family members. Social life in and around the home will be pleasant.

Mars

You may have the urge to buy or extensively rebuild a property or premises. You will put a great deal of energy into home-making. A man could become important to your home life. Guard against robbery or violence in the home.

Jupiter

This heralds a good time to run a business from your home, especially if it has an educational element. It is also a good time for financial dealings in connection with property or family matters.

Saturn

This can herald the start of a more settled phase and probably of extra responsibilities in connection with home and family life. It may be hard to bring certain aspects of your life to an end, while other things, which you would rather remained where they were, could begin to move away from you.

Uranus

A sudden move of house is possible, as are unexpected family changes. You may decide to live in an unconventional place or an unconventional manner. Your family will spring surprises on you.

Neptune

A move across or close to water is possible now. You will want your home to be a haven of artistic and creative peace. You may decide to give up a home altogether and move into some kind of unusual accommodation. Relations with your family will be different – unusual, but not necessarily unpleasant.

Pluto
Changes in relationships will affect your domestic circumstances. You may gain a home through someone else's death or give one away to others due to a birth. Sexual matters could affect your family or home situation in some way. Guard against robbery and violence in the home.

Fifth house

Mercury
You could take up a creative hobby or job that involves writing. Young people will bring pleasure.

Venus
Love, pleasure and a good time is ensured now. You may decide to work in a creative field or to express yourself in an artistic hobby. Much pleasure may be had from music, art, sex and holidays. Children bring joy and there could be a number of family celebrations now. (A Venus transit when a child is born would suggest a girl baby.)

Mars
Your love life – not to mention your sex life – could take off like a rocket now! Children may encourage you to take an interest in sporting or other active hobbies. (A Mars transit suggests that any children born now would be boys.) You may have the urge to gamble.

Jupiter
Games of chance and fun in connection with travel are on the cards now. New enterprises, marriage and childbirth should bring happiness.

Saturn
This puts a bit of a blight on romance but it can make any new relationships more serious and enduring than they otherwise might have been. This transit or progression can take some of the fun and pleasure out of your life. Responsibilities in connection with children are likely to be heavy and the love of

a child could be the cement that forces you to remain in a relationship after you have become bored with it.

Uranus

Sudden magnetic romantic attractions are probable, and separations that come about unexpectedly are another possibility. Gains and losses through speculation are likely. Unusual hobbies and holidays will attract you.

Neptune

Idealistic love is possible now and this could involve a kind of religious adoration of someone you are never likely to meet. Love of a more mundane kind is probable, but there will be hurt and confusion as a result of this. This aspect heightens creativity.

Pluto

Children may become important at this time and they may have a crucial impact on the way you live your life. Speculative enterprises could bring great wealth or great losses.

Sixth house

Mercury

This is a good time to interview staff or to look for a job. You may become interested in the plight of small animals; alternatively, hotels and convention halls may become a part of your life. Secretarial work, sales, teaching or anything else that implies communication will appeal now. You may have to deal with a health problem but this will be satisfactorily sorted out.

Venus

Women employers or employees will be pleasant to work with and female-type occupations might interest you. Creative or glamorous jobs will attract you. Your health should be good now.

Mars

You will put your back into a task and this might involve quite a bit of physical effort. You may work hard at a sporting hobby or at a do-it-yourself activity around your home. This is a good time to look for a job and then to work hard at it when you get it, but you must guard against overworking.

Jupiter

Now is a good time to find a first-rate job with the right sort of remuneration. You may choose to work in a legal or teaching field. It is also a positive time to engage staff. Your health should be good.

Saturn

This is a period of extra work and responsibility, but it will be worth the effort in the end. Older people or those who are in authority may help you. You may find your work hard, boring or uncongenial but you have to stick at it. Guard against overwork and illness.

Uranus

Sudden changes in employment and unexpected ups and downs in health occur now. Modern techniques and methods appeal to you.

Neptune

You may seek work in an artistic field or you may simply drift for a while and not bother to work at all. Allergies and other strange ailments are possible. Try to avoid sleeping pills, drugs and too much alcohol.

Pluto

If you put your heart into a job you should make money from it. You may be drawn to work in a medical or forensic field now. You will either be very well or subject to back problems and even some form of paralysis.

Seventh house

Mercury

This is a good time to sign agreements and to make partnerships. Business arrangements are more likely to be on your agenda than personal relationships, but either would go well. Enemies will come out into the open and have their say. You will find ways of communicating with others and may begin to work as an agent.

Venus

Partnerships of all kinds will bring happiness. Women colleagues will be pleasant company. Love affairs will go nicely now.

Mars

Male colleagues will be pleasant company. Partnerships of all kinds with men should go well now. You will enjoy doing things with others. You will aim for justice and fairness in your dealings, but you may go into things too quickly for your own good.

Jupiter

Legal matters will work out, as will all contractual arrangements. Money can be made from partnerships, while other benefits can accrue, such as increased knowledge and a broadening of your horizons through contacts with others.

Neptune

This is a time of either ideal love or a complete mess – or both! Business partnerships could be confusing and probably loss-making.

Pluto

A powerful drive to join others in complex financial and sexual arrangements could occur now. You may inherit or lose something through a partner's activities.

Eighth house

Mercury
Gains and losses through merging with others in business and personal relationships could take place now. You may explore and analyse your deepest feelings, especially those related to sexual matters. You could begin to read and learn about psychic matters.

Venus
Deep feelings come to the surface and you could be overtaken by your own sexual needs and the effect that another person has on these. Gains and possibly some losses through serious financial arrangements are possible. Legal matters should proceed well. You may gain through a legacy.

Mars
Births and deaths in your circle are possible. You may gain from putting your energies into a working partnership. Your sex life could take off like a rocket!

Jupiter
Karmic benefits can come your way through this progression or transit and practical benefits could come via legal matters. Financial arrangements should be good for you and for those with whom you share.

Saturn
This is the traditional sign of a death in the family, but it can also bring hardship through partnerships or other joint financial arrangements. Hard work in joint ventures can bring rewards in the end.

Uranus
Unsettled financial conditions, especially in connection with partners, can be a problem but there will be gains as well as losses. You may become involved in some kind of group activity.

Neptune

Partnership matters may become extremely confused, especially where money is concerned. You may be in danger of being swindled or led up the garden path in some way. Love relationships can be very romantic, and unwanted entanglements impossible to escape from. However, idealized love that is not at all physical in nature is also possible. Your increased sensitivity will bring psychic, healing or mediumistic ability to the fore.

Pluto

This could be wonderful or really awful. Even by transit, Pluto is likely to spend so long in this house that all the possibilities should occur sooner or later. It will bring births, deaths and changes in family and financial setups. There should be gains through legacies or other legal matters, and a good deal of money can be made on a joint venture of some kind. Your sex life could be wonderful – or a dead loss!

Ninth house

Mercury

Travel and dealings with foreigners in connection with work are likely to be beneficial, as would any course of training or study. You may become interested in religious or philosophical ideas and something that uses a *system*, such as astrology, numerology or graphology.

Venus

You may fall in love with a foreigner or move to another country as a result of meeting someone new. Contacts with people overseas or of other religions and backgrounds will be pleasant and sociable. An interest in the arts is possible. Times should be good for you now.

Mars

You may become interested in something new, especially scientific or sporting matters.

Jupiter

Everything to do with Jupiter will be emphasized, so expect benefits through foreign travel, expansion of your horizons, legal matters, religion and philosophy and all kinds of educational matters. Life should be fun and you can afford to take a gamble.

Saturn

A steady attitude to studies and to contemplative matters will take you over. If you learn anything new, you will put your mind to it. Travel in connection with older relatives is a possibility.

Uranus

You could become involved in astrology, but anything that takes your mind by storm now could change your life. Foreigners and people from different backgrounds will open your mind to new possibilities.

Neptune

Inspiration, psychic experiences and new ideas will take root in your mind. None of this may happen quickly; it is more like a long, slow change of mental direction. You will become kinder and more compassionate.

Pluto

You may receive some kind of karmic benefit. Psychic and mediumistic tendencies will surface. You may become involved with foreigners or people from a different background to your own.

Tenth house

Mercury

This should be a good time for business and career matters. Contracts and other business agreements should be worth while. You may have to give a talk or make a presentation of some kind. You will be able to discuss a few things with your family.

Venus

This is great for those who work with or for women or in a woman's field. Women may help you reach your goals. It will be easy for you to look good and to project a smooth and attractive image to the world at large.

Mars

The extra energy that Mars helps you put into your goals and ambitions can ensure that you get where you want to go. However, guard against rashness and the possibility of scandal or loss through hasty dealings.

Jupiter

This should bring honour, recognition, money and great achievements. I have seen people with such a Jupiter transit start businesses and climb the ladder of success. In a progression, this would ensure long-term success. If your goals are spiritual rather than financial or material, there is even more likelihood of success.

Saturn

The tenth house is a good place for Saturn to travel though because it keeps your nose to the grindstone and makes eventual achievement very likely. However, there may be an imbalance caused by too much focus on your aims and objectives and little left over for family life or romance. This can bring great public acclaim, or a very public downfall.

Uranus

This is an excellent aspect for astrology or any other unusual career. Computers and modern techniques would also appeal. However, goals that are charitable and humanitarian rather than material or financial in character would probably do even better.

Neptune

This could bring either great success in an artistic, psychic or other unusual field or total chaos.

Pluto
Power and the ability to change the world might be the name of the game here. It is a good placement for politics, a medical career or anything that involves investigation.

Eleventh house

Mercury
This progression or transit marks a good time to study and also to make new and interesting friends. Your ability to communicate and to project the right image increases.

Venus
Influential or wealthy friends (especially females) may enter your life, but whether they do you any good or not depends upon other factors. Social life will be terrific and friends could introduce you to the arts or to a more congenial way of life. It is possible that you will turn a friendship into a long-term love relationship.

Mars
There could be quarrels with friends but the chances are that you would prefer to expend your energies in competitive sports with your pals instead. Men friends could be very helpful in a number of unusual or unexpected ways.

Jupiter
Influential friends are a possibility but the chances are that your new companions would interest you in new and broader concepts than you had hitherto encompassed. Travel or even emigration in connection with friends is a possibility.

Saturn
Serious people and serious concerns may enter your life, and these people could help you to achieve at least one particular ambition. There could be some sorrow in connection with friends. You could join a club, society or humanitarian group for a serious purpose.

Uranus
Unusual and rather eccentric friends will enter your life. Your attitude will become more Aquarian as time goes by. You may become more interested in acquiring knowledge and in helping others than in making money. You may take up astrology or something similar.

Neptune
Artistic or creative friends may join your circle and your own desires will take a more creative turn. You could travel in connection with friends. Mysticism will attract you.

Pluto
Powerful friends could play a large part in your life style. You may do something really important for humanity. Any desire that you may have for power and status could come true in time.

Twelfth house

Mercury
Dealings with sick people and those in places of seclusion is likely. You may decide to work for the benefit of suffering humanity. Guard against signing anything or committing yourself to any important business deals without taking good care to ensure that all is as it should be. Try to avoid spilling out secrets.

Venus
You will want to help others, and this will bring karmic benefits to you in its wake. You may decide to do something to make the lives of others more pleasant. Guard against falling in love with someone totally unsuitable or having a heart-wrenching secret love affair.

Mars
Secret enemies can be a problem, while, worse still, those whom you should be able to trust could turn on you. On the other hand, you can do something positive for people who are

ill or in need of help. You may bury your anger and turn inwards or you could use this hidden energy profitably in some creative endeavour. Secret love affairs, especially those of an intense sexual nature, are possible.

Jupiter

You could put an artistic or creative talent to good measure, or you could turn to spiritual and mystical pursuits. You may seek to help others and thereby gain some kind of karmic benefit. You may have to look after confidential legal information as part of your job.

Saturn

You may be beset by shyness and uncertainty and you could choose to spend a fair bit of time alone as a result. This could be turned to an advantage by working at a creative venture over a longish period of time. You may help others, especially those who are old and sick.

Uranus

Your intuition level will increase and you may take a serious interest in astrology. You will be able to tell your friends your secrets and, in turn, you will guard their secrets for them.

Neptune

You may become a terrific musician, photographer, chiropodist or fisherman. You could have a tremendous religious conversion and you could write the definitive novel. You could, of course, break your heart over a secret lover or sacrifice all for the sake of idealistic love. You may sink into drink, drugs and degradation.

Pluto

You will become interested in the occult and in anything else that is hidden from view in some way. You may have a very intense long-term love affair which never comes out into the open. You could do much to help humanity or you may shoot yourself in the foot in some way and totally ruin your own life.

26

Planetary Aspects: the Personal Planets

Mercury

Mercury/Mercury

FAVOURABLE aspects make it easy to learn or to teach, your curiosity will be stimulated and you will need to stretch your mind. Relationships with neighbours, colleagues, brothers and sisters will be good and any local or family events will go well. You may feel like becoming a writer or journalist or taking up a job that involves sales, communication of any kind or driving.

Challenging aspects

Your mind may become temporarily blocked but this may simply lead you into other ways of thinking.

Mercury/Venus

Favourable aspects are good for business or romance – in short, anything that involves communicating with others. Social life is likely to take off and romance could well be on the cards. Negotiations and anything else to do with finances will succeed, as will any dealings with women. You will want to spend money on your appearance and this will pay off both in personal and professional life. You could become interested in art, beauty or music, and anything to do with the preparation and enjoyment of good food is well starred.

Challenging aspects

Misunderstandings with siblings, neighbours and even those you love could occur. You will find it hard to express yourself clearly, especially to those whom you love. This is the wrong time to ask for a raise or to spend money on a large scale.

Mercury/Mars

Favourable aspects speed up the mental faculties and can bring the start of a period of intense work with computers, figures and the use of good business ideas. You will think and act very quickly and can put this to good use in a business context. This should be a good time to sign papers and to work in partnership with men. Attraction to a person who shares your sporting and spare-time interests is possible. Anger and aggression can be diverted into action but you may become somewhat sarcastic and cutting. Confidence, especially in what you have to say, increases.

Challenging aspects

This is not the time to become involved in a business with others or to sign important papers. There will be disagreements over work methods and new technology may be hard to get to grips with. Anger, biting sarcasm and bitter arguments are possible. Splitting from a man either in business or personal life is possible.

Mercury/Jupiter

Pleasant aspects bring an educational phase in which you seek information and ideas on a big scale. Philosophy, religion and psychic matters will be put under the microscope and ministers of religion could enter your life. You may decide to expand business enterprises and the chances of negotiating good terms are excellent. New people in your life will open your eyes to great possibilities and travel of all kinds will be favourable. Legal matters will be successful. This is a great time to study, write or teach, and foreigners could be a source of inspiration.

Challenging aspects

You will not be able to think clearly and you may become muddled and confused about your beliefs. Conflicting ideas could confuse you. This is a bad time to become involved in legal matters or to agree to anything big that involves business negotiations. Don't sign anything important. Travel may be difficult and foreigners or foreign goods could cause problems.

Mercury/Saturn

Get the calculator out! Nice aspects make this a good time to get your head down and concentrate on a course of study or on new work practices. Anything that is started now should be finished properly in due course. Nothing will happen quickly but progress will be made. This progression will probably be most useful to those people who are over 40 because it is then that Saturn seems to be at its most comfortable. A realistic and methodical approach will pay off and there may be an interest in scientific or detailed work of some kind. Older people may be influential in business matters and an older relative could help you out. Family matters will be sorted out and there could be some travel to and from family members or on business.

Challenging aspects

You may feel tongue tied and stupid at this time but, if you can get over this phase or find a way of expressing yourself, you can make use of it. Try not to lose your fragile grip on your confidence. Hard work, especially in a scientific field, can bring results, and writing may be especially successful. Guard against problems that arise through sloppy financial or business practices and also against overworking or allowing a health problem to get out of hand.

Mercury/Uranus

Pleasant aspects will stimulate your mind and take you into new realms of thought. Original and unusual ideas can be successfully pursued. Computers, astrology, science and other modern techniques will appeal to you, while teaching and studying are other possibilities. You should make new friends and become involved in institutions, groups and social clubs that are stimulating and amusing. A new job or a new way of doing a current one are possible. You may become involved in alternative therapies and spiritual healing and your intuition level will increase dramatically.

Challenging aspects

Something could suddenly go wrong and hitherto reliable machinery will be taken over by gremlins. You may have some very original ideas but they may be too far out to be realistic. Your temper and your mental processes will be erratic and uncertain. There may be arguments with neighbours and siblings and you could be the one who sets these off. You will have to take care while driving or travelling around your locality for some time now.

Mercury/Neptune

A happy aspect between Mercury and Neptune means that you could fall in love with a dream or a vision that does not match up to reality but which is delightful while it lasts! If it isn't love that fascinates you, it will be the spiritual side of life that appeals. You will find it easier to visualize and to conceptualize at this time. Dreams may become reality now and travel near or over water will be beneficial. This is a great time to put creative ideas into action and hobbies such as acting could prove to be fun.

Challenging aspects

If you fall in love with a dream or a vision now, you could be in for a rude awakening later on! Guard against becoming involved with deceitful people, losers, betrayers or those who seek to destroy your confidence. Drinkers and drugtakers may be tremendously appealing but they are all part of the illusion. There may be scandal, loss and difficulties in dealing with people in business or legal matters. Try not to travel or become involved with foreigners for the time being if you can avoid it. Psychic or psychological problems may arise. Anything mentioned in the happy aspect section could go wrong now, but if it does try not to be too hard on yourself. We *all* make mistakes, especially when Neptune is around!

Mercury/Pluto

Beneficial aspects between these two planets bring an increased interest in business or other partnerships that are concerned with shared resources or merging with others in any way. You will want to look behind and beneath every question and it will be easy for you to solve mysteries now. This would be a great time to write a successful thriller! You may take an interest in psychic matters and you will want to know how these work. You will want to improve your education and probably your financial position as well. You will be able to communicate with others on many levels. There could be legal dealings, possibly as a result of deaths in the family, and siblings may well be involved in these matters. You will want to look into matters relating to birth, death and sex!

Challenging aspects

Something could go wrong in business and legal matters could become a minefield. You may even have to pay someone to investigate a particular problem or a situation. This is not a good time to sign anything important and you should take care over matters relating to taxes, mortgages and so on. Try to avoid becoming involved in strange psychic experiences or practices. There may be difficulties in connection with siblings and neighbours. Anything mentioned in the favourable aspect section could go wrong now. Sexual matters may be difficult and you may even become prey to an obscene phone caller!

Mercury/Chiron

Chiron could be a second ruler of Virgo and thus very comfortable when in happy aspect to Mercury. Excellent aspects bring a great time to study and to teach and also to take up any interest in health or healing. Sporting interests would be favourable (I mean *playing* sports, not betting on them!). If you or any member of your family has been ill lately, they will soon recover.

Challenging aspects

Health is the big problem here and any ailment that occurs now could hang around for a long time. Studying, teaching and sporting interests could be problematical. Take care of any sick people who are around you.

Mercury/nodes

Depending upon the node that is involved, nice aspects suggest that past experiences or completely new ideas could be very successful. Anything that you do now will fit well with the public mood, and any form of public relations or image polishing would be a great success. Property and family dealings will succeed.

Challenging aspects

Basically all the ideas mentioned above would be losers for a while.

Mercury/ascendant

Your confidence is on the increase and your sense of initiative and enterprise is building all the time. Your communications ability will be developing and all business matters should go well.

Challenging aspects

Guard against overexpansion in business and watch what you agree to. Try to think before you speak and not to allow others to sap your confidence.

Mercury/midheaven

A great time for business enterprises or for forging ahead in any sphere of life that requires communication ability. A career change or an alteration in your direction is quite likely. If you deserve a raise or a promotion, ask for it now.

Challenging aspects

Difficulties in connection with your aims and ambitions are likely to arise.

Venus

Venus/Venus

This is a very romantic aspect which could lead you to fall in love! You will appreciate music, art and beauty in all its forms. Women could be very helpful to you and life should be easy and pleasant. It will be simple to make money and very agreeable to spend it. People in your circle will be friendly, helpful and sociable and you will be able to impress them with your charm and charisma.

Challenging aspects

There could be difficulties in connection with money or relationships.

Venus/Mars

A love affair could be on the cards and, if so, this would be very romantic and also very sexy. This is a time to spend money on a few little luxuries and also on pleasing your lover. You might take an active interest in artistic or creative pursuits.

Challenging aspects

Guard against allowing your feelings to run away with you and don't allow greedy people to use you as a meal ticket.

Venus/Jupiter

This could be a real money-spinner and you can afford to take a gamble. You should be able to enjoy whatever you are doing, either in a social or a career context. The culture and benefits of those with whom you come into contact will influence you beneficially. There may be travel in connection with business.

Challenging aspects

Overexpansion could lead to losses. Travel may be expensive.

Venus/Saturn

Creative ventures may be slow going but, once the work has been put into them, they should be successful. Friendships and acquaintanceships will be rather pleasant and relationships with older relatives will also be nice. This is a difficult time for love relationships because, on one hand, they could become durable now but, on the other hand, they may bring trials and tribulations in their wake.

Challenging aspects
This could mark a difficult time for all relationships.

Venus/Uranus
Sudden attractions are possible and any love affair that occurs at this time will be 'too hot not to cool down', as the old song says. New friendships and exciting people and experiences are likely now and life will be pleasantly unpredictable. Work that involves electronics could prove to be viable.

Challenging aspects
You may fall for the wrong person, become involved in the wrong job or find the wrong kind of friends. You may be eased out of a position in a group or an organization.

Venus/Neptune
This is a really dreamy and romantic phase in which you are almost bound to fall in love with something or someone. The trouble is that you will put your lover on a pedestal and not be able to see reality for the mists of romance. This is a good time to be compassionate and charming towards others.

Challenging aspects
Romance could go wrong and losses can occur in business. Avoid the drugs, sex and rock-and-roll scene if you can!

Venus/Pluto
Powerful feelings will become apparent and you could find yourself falling into a very intense love affair at this time. You may make a great deal of money from some kind of peculiar or hidden source and you could even inherit wealth.

Challenging aspects
Watch your heart and your bank account!

Venus/Chiron

You should be feeling well, and if anyone around you has been ill they should begin to recover. A woman may teach you something useful.

Challenging aspects

Chiron aspects can be difficult as far as health, restriction and relationships are concerned, so take care.

Venus/nodes

This is a good time to spend money on property and to go into something that the public will appreciate. You may fall in love with someone to whom you feel karmically drawn.

Challenging aspects

You may be drawn to something or someone who is wrong for you.

Venus/ascendant

A good time to make a start on improving your image, your appearance and your finances. You will become happier and easier to get along with. You may begin to look for someone to love or you could get involved in something creative.

Challenging aspects

There could be relationship difficulties and a loss of the creative urge.

Venus/midheaven

This is a great time to forge ahead with your aims and ambitions, and there could be money to be made. Romance could lead to business opportunities or, alternatively, you could meet someone pleasant through your job. You will look good and feel good about yourself, and maintain excellent relations with parents, bosses and older people.

Challenging aspects

Life becomes a bit of grind and rather boring for a while.

Mars

Mars/Mars

This marks the start of a very busy phase in which you can get a great deal done. Your energy level will be high and you will be happy to rush about and do everything at great speed. Jobs that are traditionally considered to be masculine, such as engineering, car maintenance and building, may become part of your life now.

Challenging aspects

Guard against rashness and accidents through handling sharp objects in a hasty manner. Take care while driving.

Mars/Jupiter

This brings an expansion in all business, money-making or cultural affairs. Travel, either in connection with business or in order to explore new faces and places, is well starred now. Groups or organizations that are involved in religion, astrology or spiritual matters might appeal to you.

Challenging aspects

Guard against overexpansion in any area of your life and take care while travelling. Avoid dealing with aggressive men.

Mars/Saturn

You can forge ahead very successfully with this aspect because the energy of Mars is directed and controlled by Saturn. Progress in career matters and an increase in status are possible. Older people, those in authority or men in general may help you at this time. You may find yourself dealing in a beneficial way with people who wear uniforms or who work in the fields of engineering or science.

Challenging aspects

You may find it hard to achieve your ambitions and there may be people who try to stand in your way. You could become resentful and angry and lose your temper as a result.

Mars/Uranus

This may be too much of a good thing because your emotions may be hard to control. A hectic love affair is possible now. You could take advantage of this progression or transit by putting your heart into new and original ideas. You could take up some form of self-improvement, perhaps a sport or a course of education or training. Your confidence level should increase.

Challenging aspects

Guard against accidents or losses through hasty behaviour. Arguments are more than likely at this time.

Mars/Neptune

Your psychic powers and intuition will be on the increase and you could meet people who inspire you to take an interest in spiritual matters at this time. If you are interested in any kind of creative endeavour, this will begin to go very well. Behind-the-scenes work or any selfless help that you give to others will be worth while.

Challenging aspects

You could fall in love with the wrong type of person, become obsessed with them and get hurt as a result. Your sexual drive is very high and it could lead you into some really peculiar behaviour. Avoid drink, drugs and the lower levels of life if you can.

Mars/Pluto

You will want to push things to the limit and your increased will-power will enable you to do so. You may reach a position of influence or power. This is an excellent time to deal with business matters, especially those that involve joint finances. Sexual and relationship matters could be spectacular.

Challenging aspects

Power struggles and temper tantrums are possible. Try to avoid political situations or places that could put you in a dangerous position. Business matters and relationships with others could be frustrating due to power struggles. Sex could cause some kind of major problem in your life.

Mars/Chiron

You may be driven to help those who are sick and you may even train in some form of medicine or healing. You may study or teach some kind of sports or you may find a mentor for your more spiritual interests.

Challenging aspects

Guard against accidents and look after yourself.

Mars/nodes

This is a good time for property dealings. You may get together with family members and either plan for the future or reminisce about the past. Anything that you take up now will be well received by the public and there may be a karmic benefit from the good that you have done in the past. Life is easy for a change.

Challenging aspects

There may be family and domestic difficulties and a feeling that you are swimming against the tide.

Mars/ascendant

This is a time to break out of your rut and make a fresh start. You will be more self-centred but this is probably no bad thing.

Challenging aspects

It is hard to get anything off the ground now and you may be feeling off-colour. People could be awkward and obstreperous.

Mars/midheaven

This is a good time to put your energies into getting on and making achievements. A man may help you reach your goals. Try to rest if you can because the chances are that you are working very hard at this time. If you want a rise or a promotion, ask for it now.

Challenging aspects

Someone may stand in the way of your progress and there could be a series of frustrating arguments as a result of this. It is not a good time to approach anyone for a rise or for anything else that you want.

27

Planetary Aspects: the Transpersonal and Impersonal Planets

YOU ARE UNLIKELY to have to deal with these planets in the day-for-a-year type of progression, but they will occur in other forms of progression and transit.

To find the effect of the challenging aspects, simply turn each interpretation on its head. This glimpse into the movements of the planets is not really deep enough, but it will give you something to hang your hat on until you can read more or study plenty of charts.

Jupiter

Jupiter/Jupiter

This will bring new opportunities and an expansion of your horizons. Legal affairs go well, as do educational and spiritual matters. It is also a good time to travel.

Jupiter/Saturn

Now is a good time to expand cautiously, especially in speculative ventures. Older people or those who have a spiritual outlook may be helpful.

Jupiter/Uranus

This is a time of massive expansion. Original and unusual

people and ideas can lead you into new directions. Unexpected luck could come your way. It is also a good time to deal with governments and politics in general.

Jupiter/Neptune
Travel over or near water would be favourable. Expansion of ideas, especially spiritual and mystical ones, will be interesting and successful. Healing and mediumship would be especially attractive at this time. Money can be made from creative endeavours.

Jupiter/Pluto
Spiritual matters will come to the fore now and you should experience an increase in your level of intuition. You may develop an interest in health and healing or in legal matters.

Jupiter/nodes
Luck is on the cards in connection with property, family life or work that affects the public, or some form of karmic benefit.

Jupiter/ascendant
Here is a fresh start with everything to play for. There will be a great expansion of horizons.

Jupiter/midheaven
This could be a terrific time for all career matters. Progress may be fast or slow but it is ensured. You may find a spiritual belief that changes your life for the better.

Saturn

Saturn/Saturn
This is a time of facing reality. Your life may change for better or for worse, but there will be a period of hard work and of sorting yourself out on an inner level.

Saturn/Uranus
This represents a push/pull situation in which Uranus wants to forge ahead and Saturn puts on the brakes. You will become

noticed by others and you could achieve a strong position in something political. You will be able to put modern techniques to good use, and a realistic attitude to original ideas could bring wonderful rewards. You will take responsibility in some kind of group activity and friends will become an important part of your life.

Saturn/Neptune

Secret projects can be worked on successfully and you may tap into your spiritual or intuitive abilities in a useful manner. Creative enterprises will be hard work but they can be brought to fruition. Love affairs can prosper under this progression or transit, and they would combine common sense and idealistic romance.

Saturn/Pluto

Your concentration will increase and there is a good chance of making progress in some large project that involves big and authoritative organizations. Ambitions can come to the surface and be achieved.

Saturn/nodes

Steady progress can be made at home. The political or prevailing situation in your environment will help you to achieve your ambitions. There may be some karmic benefit from way back in the past or even from a past life.

Saturn/ascendant

This can be a time of progress if you are prepared to work hard and to concentrate on details. You may become rather shy and withdrawn or so devoted to your ambitions that you forget to follow up on love and family life.

Saturn/midheaven

People in authority can help you now. You should forge ahead with your ambitions but try to avoid becoming cold and hard.

Uranus

Uranus/Uranus

This is a time of revolution when you break out from your mould. Friends may exert a strong influence on your life now. Original and unusual ideas will attract you and you may become unpredictable and eccentric for a while. Astrology will appeal.

Uranus/Neptune

Mysticism, astrology and the desire to learn characterize this aspect. You could become caught up in almost anything that is other-worldly. If afflicted, guard against drink or drugs.

Uranus/Pluto

Major changes that are happening out in the world could affect your life style in a major way. You could change direction radically and leave just about anything or everything behind in order to start again. Powerful feelings come to the surface.

Uranus/nodes

You could develop an interest in astrology or spiritual matters. Friends will influence your life in some way and there may be a fated or karmic feel to all this. You may take up politics or something else that involves the public.

Uranus/ascendant

A complete change of life style is probable. You may break out of your mould and leave some meaningful part of your being behind. Groups of people and friends will have an important bearing on your life. You may become interested in astrology or something similar.

Uranus/midheaven

A change of job or a complete alteration of direction is likely. You may become attracted to electronics, astrology, computers or other modern techniques. Working with friends or in a political or humanitarian sphere is likely.

Neptune

Neptune/Neptune

This is a good time for creative projects or to indulge yourself in art, photography, film or anything else that creates an illusion. You may fall in love and you won't be able to see straight as a result. You may come to terms with something that went wrong in your past.

Neptune/Pluto

Some kind of major change is affecting your life. This could be a political or world situation but it can also impinge on your personal life. You may fall in love, take up an artistic career or change your life entirely in some way.

Neptune/nodes

You may decide to move your home close to the sea or to a source of water. Love could affect your life style, your job and your family situation. You may do something for others that leads to karmic benefits in the future.

Neptune/ascendant

A dreamy time is on the way and this could lead to an increase in your spirituality or creativity. You may fall in love or become a prey to illusions. Film, photography or other Neptunian pursuits may be important.

Neptune/midheaven

A career in an artistic field is likely. You may become interested in cosmetics, hairdressing, film, photography or art. You may fall in love with someone whom you meet through work.

Pluto

Pluto/Pluto

You may appear to change your life suddenly, but the chances are that this change has been on the way for years.

Pluto/nodes

A change of address and a change of family circumstances is possible. You may seek to influence events now or you may be influenced by the prevailing political situation. Karmic benefits might be on the way.

Pluto/ascendant

A change of direction is likely, with you taking a grip on your life and on your surrounding circumstances. You may feel paralyzed and unable to make changes, but subtle alterations are going on somewhere deep down inside you. You could take an interest in big business or in shared or joint ventures.

Pluto/midheaven

This is a terrific time for influencing the world that you live in. Political or other situations may give you opportunities for advancement. You will have to deal with taxes, corporate matters and anything that arises through joint financial matters.

Nodes

Nodes/ascendant/descendant

It is hard to quantify the changes that this kind of aspect brings, but it is bound to affect you personally and also those around you. Something out in the world could affect your life beneficially and there could be fated or karmic events of various kinds. Changes in relationships could be beneficial or otherwise at this time.

Nodes/midheaven/nadir

Changes in direction are likely. You may change your address or your job, and there seems to be a karmic or fated feel to all this. You could experience alterations in your family situation, especially in connection with older relatives. A transformation in the political or environmental atmosphere will be beneficial (or otherwise) to you in some way.

Index